BOOKBINDING THE TRADITIONAL WAY

A CLASSIC MANUAL FOR METHODS AND
EQUIPMENT IN BOOK MAKING, BINDERY,
AND COVER FINISHING

BY **PAUL N. HASLUCK**

ORIGINALLY PUBLISHED IN 1902

LEGACY EDITION

HASLUCK'S TRADITIONAL SKILLS LIBRARY
BOOK 4

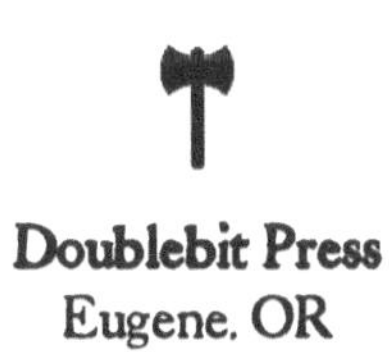

Doublebit Press
Eugene, OR

INTRODUCTION
To The Doublebit Press Legacy Edition

The old experts of artisanal trades, country and homestead knowledge, and the woods and mountains taught timeless principles and skills for centuries. Through their timeless books, the old experts offered rich descriptions of how the world works and encouraged learning through personal experiences *by doing.* Over the last 125 years, manufacturing, farming, and construction have substantially changed. Of course, many things have gotten simpler as equipment and technology have improved. In addition, some activities of pre-digital times are now no longer in vogue, or are even outright considered inappropriate or illegal. However, despite many of the positive changes in manufacturing and crafting methods that have occurred over the years, *there are many other skills and much knowledge that have been forgotten.*

By publishing *The Hasluck Traditional Skills Library*, it is our goal at Doublebit Press to do what we can to preserve and share the works from forgotten teachers that form the cornerstone of the history of the American artisans and traditional crafts. Through remastered reprint editions of timeless classics, perhaps we can regain some of this lost knowledge for future generations.

This book is an important contribution traditional handcraft and country skills literature and has important historical and collector value toward preserving the American handcraft and outdoors tradition. The knowledge it holds is an invaluable reference for practicing skills and hand craft methods. Its chapters thoroughly discuss some of the essential building blocks of knowledge that are fundamental but may have been forgotten as equipment gets fancier and technology gets smarter. In short, this book was chosen for Legacy Edition printing because much of the basic skills and knowledge it contains has been forgotten or put to the wayside in trade for more modern conveniences and methods.

With technology playing a major role in everyday life, sometimes we need to take a step back in time to find those basic building blocks used for gaining mastery – the things that we have luckily not completely lost and has been recorded in books over the last two centuries. These skills aren't forgotten, they've just been shelved. *It's time to unshelve them once again and reclaim the lost knowledge of self-sufficiency.*

Based on this commitment to preserving our outdoors and handcraft artisanal heritage, we have taken great pride in publishing this book as a complete original work. We hope it is worthy of both study and collection by outdoors folk in the modern era of outdoors and traditional skills life.

Unlike many other photocopy reproductions of classic books that are common on the market, this Legacy Edition does not simply place poor photography of old texts on our pages and use error-prone optical scanning or computer-generated text. We want our work to speak for itself, and reflect the quality demanded by our customers who spend their hard-earned money. With this in mind, each Legacy Edition book that has been chosen for publication is carefully remastered from original print books, *with the Doublebit Legacy Edition printed and laid out in the exact way that it was presented at its original publication.* We provide a beautiful, memorable experience that is as true to the original text as best as possible, but with the aid of modern technology to make as beautiful a reading experience as possible for books that can be over a century old.

Because of its age and because it is presented in its original form, the book may contain misspellings, inking errors from print plates, and other printing blemishes that were common for the age. However, these are exactly the things that we feel give the book its character, which we preserved in this Legacy Edition. During digitization, we ensured that each illustration in the text was clean and sharp with the least amount of loss from being copied and digitized as possible. Full-page plate illustrations are presented as they were found, often including the extra blank page that was often behind a plate. For the covers, we use the original cover design to give the book its original feel. We are sure you'll appreciate the fine touches and attention to detail that your Legacy Edition has to offer.

For traditional handcrafters and classic artisanal enthusiasts who demand the best from their equipment, this Doublebit Press Legacy Edition reprint was made with you in mind. Both important and minor details have equally both been accounted for by our publishing staff, down to the cover, font, layout, and images. It is the goal of Doublebit Legacy Edition series to be worthy of collection in any outdoorsperson's library and that can be passed to future generations.

Every book selected to be in this series offers unique views and instruction on important skills, advice, tips, tidbits, anecdotes, stories, and experiences that will enrichen the repertoire of any person who enjoys escaping a bit from today's modern technology-based, cookie-cutter, and highly industrialized skills. Instead, folks seeking to make things with their hands like the old days may find great value from these resurrected instructional manuals from the past. These books were not simply written to be shelved in a library – they contain our history and forgotten methods to make things with real character and energy with a *human* component.

Therefore, to learn the most basic building blocks of a craft leads to mastery of all its aspects. We hope this book helps you along this path with its rich descriptions and illustrations!

About Hasluck's Traditional Skills Library

Paul N. Hasluck was a prominent author on artisan skills and traditional handcrafts toward the end of the 19th Century. He was the editor of the magazine *Work*, which was a popular handcraft, shop skills, and artisanal craft magazine of the day. His broad expertise in making things with your hands led him to write or edit over 30 volumes on specific handcrafts, arts, and mechanics, with each manual containing invaluable information related to each craft.

Hasluck had a great eye for collecting the info that beginners and experts alike needed to perfect their craft. His volumes were loaded with helpful diagrams, tables, and illustrations that are useful even by today's digital standards. In short, Hasluck's instructional manuals were the *go-to instructional library* if someone wanted to learn a particular skill. Used by the U.S. military, the Boy and Girl Scouts, and countless folks at farms, public libraries, and homes across the world, Hasluck's instructional manuals were the perfect "handy book" for learning.

This Doublebit Press Legacy Edition republishes this tradition of handcrafted quality and artisanal work. We hope that this deluxe printed edition of this work will help you gain mastery in your craft, as it is presented in the exact form that it was originally published. Even today, the knowledge contained within its pages are timeless and have much to teach!

Finally, as art, Hasluck's manuals contain beautiful illustrations and line art that are a sign of simpler, yet authentic times when quality mattered and craftsmanship was king. This collectible volume makes a great addition to the bookshelf of any handcrafter, maker, artisan, farmer, homesteader, or outdoors enthusiast!

BOOKBINDING

WITH NUMEROUS ENGRAVINGS AND DIAGRAMS

EDITED BY

PAUL N. HASLUCK

EDITOR OF "WORK" AND "BUILDING WORLD,"
AUTHOR OF "HANDYBOOKS FOR HANDICRAFTS," ETC. ETC.

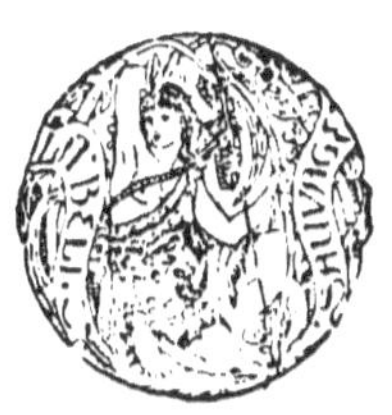

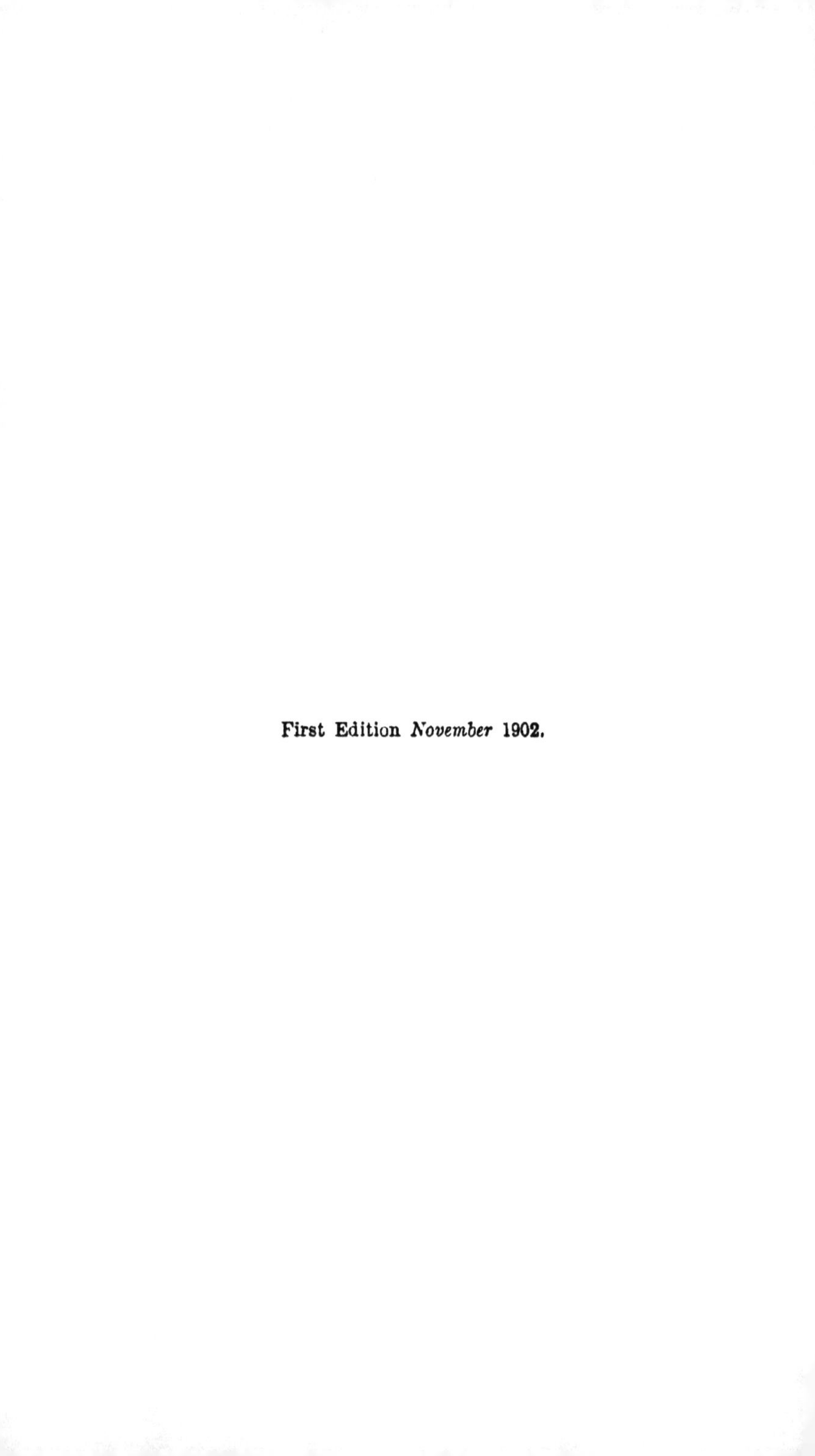

First Edition *November* 1902.

PREFACE.

THIS Handbook contains, in a form convenient for everyday use, a comprehensive digest of the information on Bookbinding, scattered over nearly twenty thousand columns of WORK—one of the weekly journals it is my fortune to edit—and supplies concise information on the details of the subjects of which it treats.

In preparing for publication in book form the mass of relevant matter contained in the volumes of WORK, much had to be arranged anew, altered, and largely rewritten. The contributions of many are so blended that the writings of individuals cannot be distinguished for acknowledgment. A large part of the contents was written by the Foreman Bookbinder in a London firm, and the substance of a series of articles written by Mr. Wm. Norman Brown has also been incorporated.

Readers who may desire additional information respecting special details of the matters dealt with in this Handbook, or instructions on kindred subjects, should address a question to WORK, so that it may be answered in the columns of that journal.

P. N. HASLUCK.

La Belle Sauvage, London.

CONTENTS.

BOOKBINDING.

CHAPTER I.

BOOKBINDERS' APPLIANCES.

BOOKBINDING is a term that is popularly applied to any process for making a book by fastening together printed or unprinted sheets of paper, and providing them in this compact form with a suitable covering. The term, used in this sense, covers such widely different productions as a cheap cloth- or paper-covered novel and a costly volume bound in leather. These two books are representative products of the two great divisions of the bookbinding industry as carried on at the present day. Each division may, indeed, almost be called a distinct industry ; for, though the means employed and the results obtained in both cases bear on the surface a certain resemblance to each other, the manner in which the work is carried out, and the result aimed at, are in both cases fundamentally different.

A bound book is, technically, a book bound in leather. It is more solid in appearance, is better sewn, the leaves lie more compactly together, and the book opens more readily than a cloth-boarded book. Even a person without any technical knowledge is struck with the difference between a leather-bound volume and a cloth-boarded book. While the former will last for years and resist hard usage, the latter serves a temporary purpose only, and rough usage soon reduces it to a collection of loose leaves, scarcely held together by a few tangled threads. Belonging also to the division of bound

books are half-bound books, of which the back may
be of leather, or of cloth or other material used in
place of leather, and the sides of cloth or paper.
Other minor but not unimportant differences that
distinguish bound books from cloth-boarded books
will be explained in due course.

The tools used in bookbinding first will be
described. A cloth-boarded book can be produced
with the same tools (though less in number) that
are employed for a leather-bound volume, but the
latter cannot be produced with the appliances used
for the former.

Before beginning the study of this subject, the
amateur is advised to obtain two old leather-bound

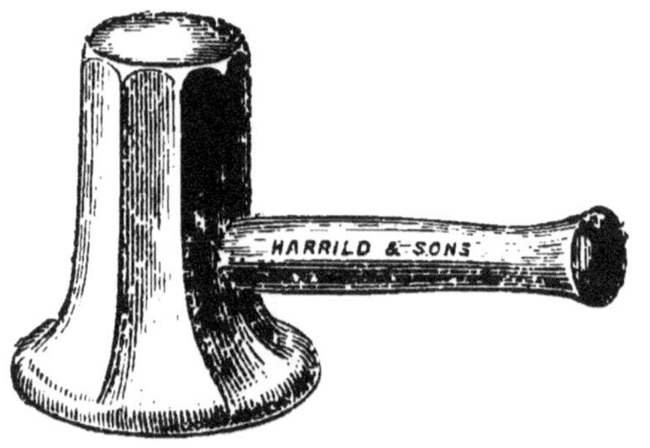

Fig. 1.—Beating Hammer.

books. Take one of these books to pieces carefully,
bit by bit; and whilst doing so note every contrivance used for holding the book together, and frequently compare the partially dissected book with
the other volume, which should be kept intact. The
value of this object lesson will be realised when
making the first attempt at binding a book.

A book may be bound by the amateur with the
aid of comparatively few and simple tools. It has
not, therefore, been thought necessary to describe
here the many more or less expensive machines and
appliances at present used in bookbinding. Leather
binding is largely done by hand, the material em-

ployed, the manner in which the work is done, and the limited demand for leather compared with cloth books, precluding the use of machinery to any considerable extent. On the other hand, the binding of cloth-boarded books is considerably helped, and, in some cases, almost wholly done, by machinery; because cloth books must be produced rapidly, and in large numbers (often tens of thousands, all of one size and pattern), and at a comparatively low cost.

The following are some of the tools that will be required for leather binding :—

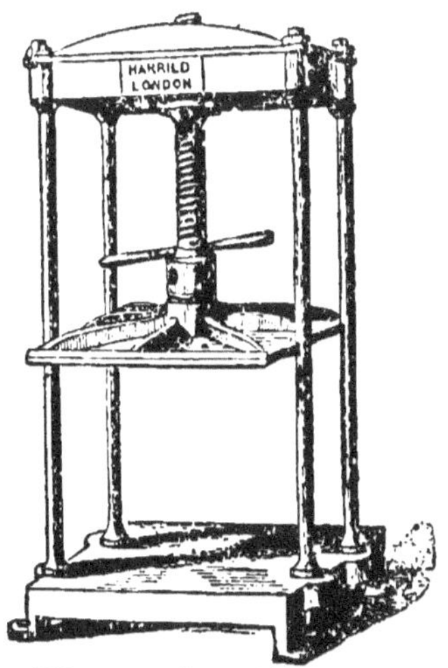

Fig. 2.—Standing Press.

The folder or folding-stick is a piece of flat bone, about 6 in. long and rather more than 1 in. wide, with rounded ends. The folder, as its name implies, is used for folding into page size the printed sheets received from the printer.

The beating hammer and stone are adjuncts of an old-fashioned bookbinder's shop, and have been replaced by the rolling machine. The amateur, however, unless he can get his work rolled for him, must use the beating hammer, and he should endeavour to obtain one that has been specially made

for the purpose. The beating hammer weighs from
10 lb. to 12 lb., is more or less bell-shaped, and has a
short handle (see Fig. 1, p. 10). A stone or iron slab
will also be required. The slab must be level and
perfectly smooth, and it should be firmly bedded.
When not in use the surface of the slab should be
kept covered. It will be found convenient to bed the
slab in a box of sand, and to provide the box with
a cover.

The standing press is used to compress books
during the process of binding, and there are several

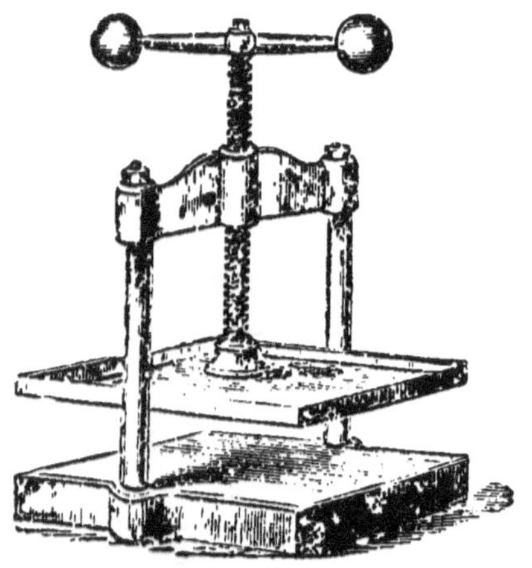

Fig. 3.—Simple Press.

different forms of it. The typical standing press
(Fig. 2, p. 11) consists of vertical pillars; a long stout
screw, a platen, and the bed. A letter-copying
press represents, roughly and on a small scale, a
bookbinder's standing press, but in the bookbinder's
press the power is applied by a long iron bar that
is inserted in holes drilled in a ball of iron that
forms the bottom of the screw. The folded sections
of the book are piled upon the bed of the press,
and the platen is screwed down as tightly as
possible by the combined strength of two or more
men. A stout copying press, however, can be used

for bookbinding on a small scale, smooth slabs of iron or hard wood called pressing boards, not less than the size of the book, being placed between each three or four sections. Or, if a copying press or similar contrivance is not available, heavy weights may be laid on the folded sheets, and the pressure continued for twenty-four hours, or longer if necessary. A small press, like that shown by

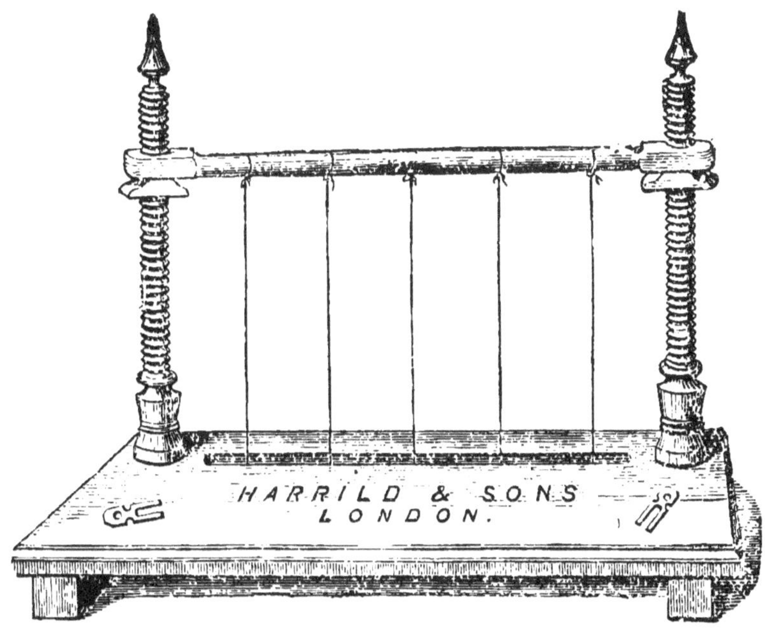

Fig. 4.—Sewing Press.

Fig. 3, sometimes may be bought second-hand, and would be a valuable acquisition. The pressing boards should be of some hard wood, generally beech, planed perfectly smooth on both surfaces, and rectangular in shape. Iron plates sometimes are used.

The sewing press is not a press in the modern sense of the term, as it is not used for purposes of compression ; it is a contrivance by which the bands or cords upon which a book is sewn are kept at tension and in their proper places, while the sections or sheets of a book are sewn to them. The usual form of the sewing press is shown by Fig. 4, p. 13, and its use will be described later. In Fig. 4 are shown the keys employed to hold down the cords.

A home-made sewing press is illustrated by Fig. 5. The bottom board A may be made of 1-in. stuff, 1 ft. 9 in. long by 1 ft. broad, with uprights c, 10 in. high by 1¼ in. by ¾ in. The top piece B, shown separately in Fig. 6, should be of 1-in. oak, 2 ft. 3 in. long, 1 in. square, with corners rounded, and

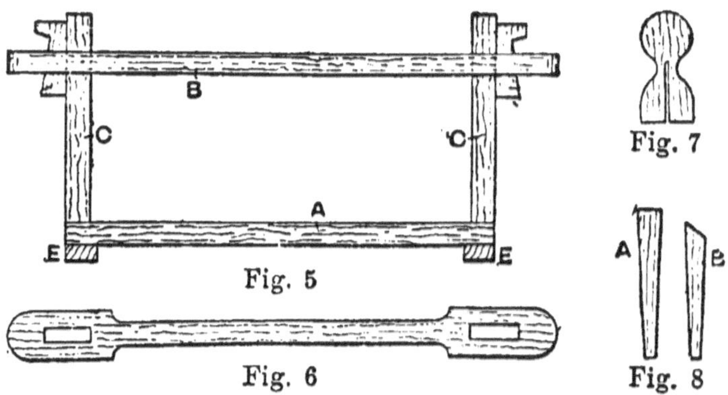

Fig. 5

Fig. 6

Fig. 7

Fig. 8

Figs. 5 to 8.—Details of Home-made Sewing Press.

2¼ in. wide at the ends. The cross-pieces E underneath measure 1½ in. by ¾ in. The uprights can be either hinged or fixed with iron plates screwed on from outside. The key (Fig. 7) is of ⅜-in. ash, cut to the shape shown, 2½ in. long, 1¼ in. wide, and ½ in. wide in the middle, and with a saw-cut for the string. Three keys are wanted. The cutting and backing boards (sections of which are shown at A and B in Fig. 8) can be 1 ft. 3 in. long by 3½ in. wide.

Another sewing press is shown by Fig. 9. It is simply a flat bottom with two screwed uprights, and cross-bar with nuts below for the purpose of keeping the bands or strings tight while the book is being sewn. The slit immediately below the crossbar and between the uprights allows of strings going through and being fastened on the bottom with a tack or anything handy. A wooden screw upright is preferable, and the ends need not be glued into the bottom, but fitted so that they can be taken out for convenience, and the whole stowed away in small compass. Differing only in detail is the sewing press illustrated by Fig. 10, p. 16.

The lying press (Fig. 11, p. 16) (more commonly called the laying press) may also be termed the back-

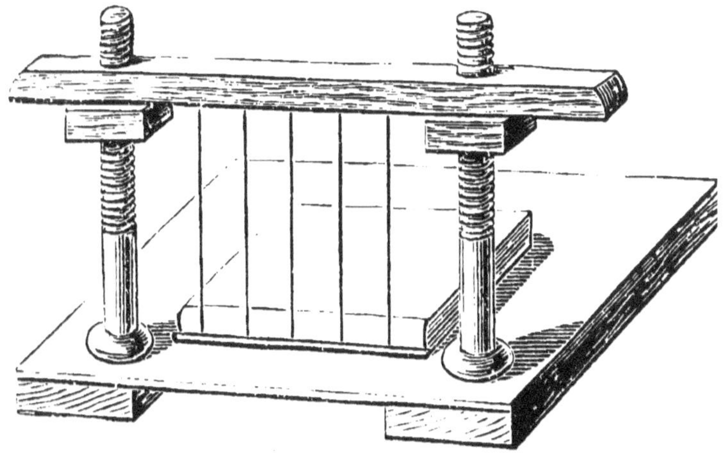

Fig. 9.—Sewing Press.

ing press and the cutting press, as both the operations of backing a book and of cutting the edges are performed at it. For cutting, is kept uppermost the side that has on the left cheek the two guide rods between which the plough works, as shown at Fig. 12, p. 17. For backing, the press is turned over, and the plain sides of the cheeks are placed uppermost. This press is worked by a short unattached iron press pin.

A lying press of slightly different construction is illustrated by Fig. 13, p. 18, which shows a plough,

A, in position also. The construction of this particular plough will be dealt with later. This press consists of six essential parts—two boards, two screws,

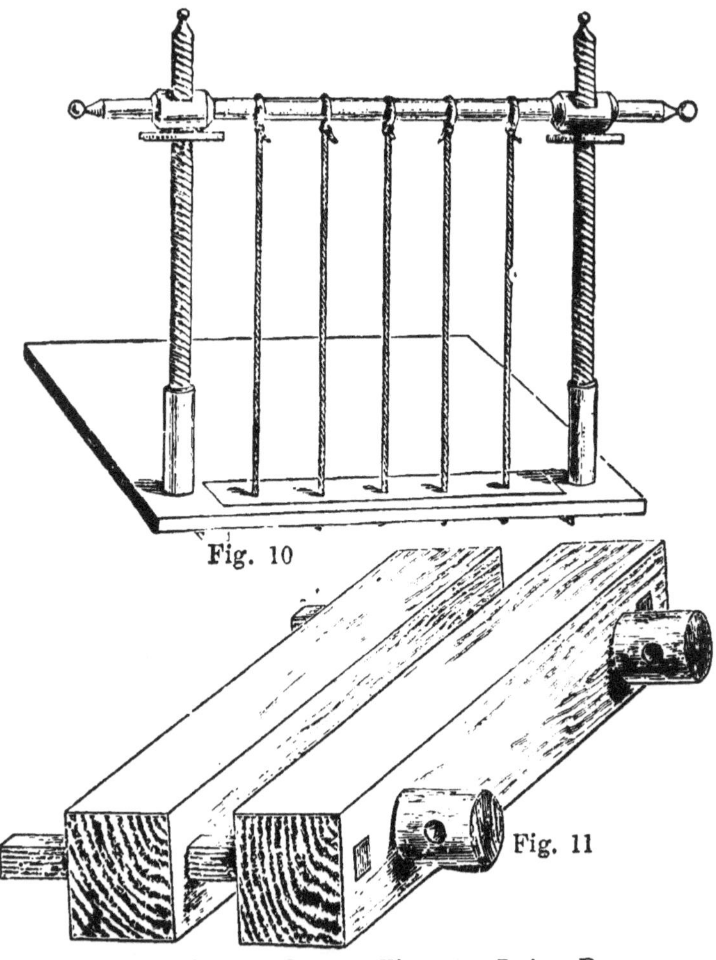

Fig. 10

Fig. 11

Fig. 10.—Sewing Press. Fig. 11.—Lying Press.

and two drilled and tapped handles. To make it, first procure a piece of board 18 in. long, 6 in. broad, and 1½ in. thick; then get another one of the same length and thickness, but only 5½ in. broad. Plane these perfectly true and fasten

together temporarily, with two faces together and
one long edge of each piece flush with that of the
other, and bore a hole right through for the screw,
which must now be made. The screw may be of
wood, similar to the screw of a carpenter's vice; but
an iron one answers the purpose quite as well.
Threaded pieces of iron wire ($\frac{3}{8}$ in. or $\frac{5}{16}$ in.), about
8 in. long, have one end each screwed into a plate
of iron 1 in. or 2 in. across, either round or square,

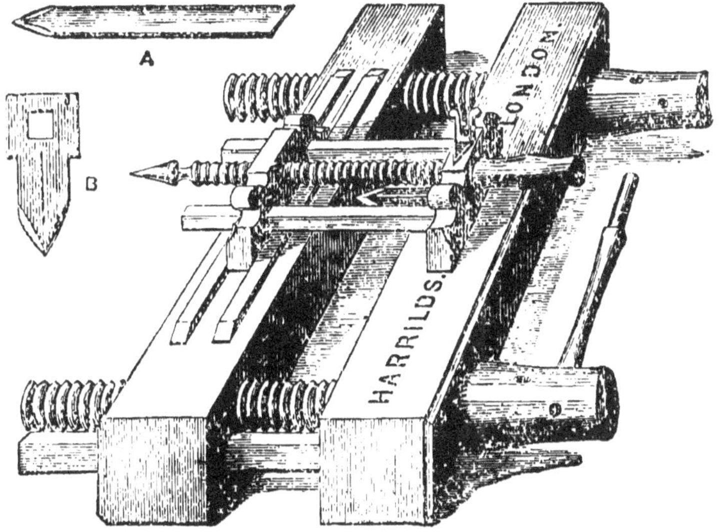

Fig. 12.—Lying Press.

and about $\frac{1}{8}$ in. thick (see Fig. 14, p. 18); the end of
the screw is burred over to hold more firmly. The
iron or brass handles are tapped sufficiently large to
allow them to be screwed on with comparative
ease; a lever on each one enables sufficient power
to be obtained to press the books well together.
Having fitted together the parts of the screw, take
off the handles, and pass the screw through the
back board, and fasten it in place by passing small
screws through the holes in the plate. These screws
will keep the large screw from slipping backwards

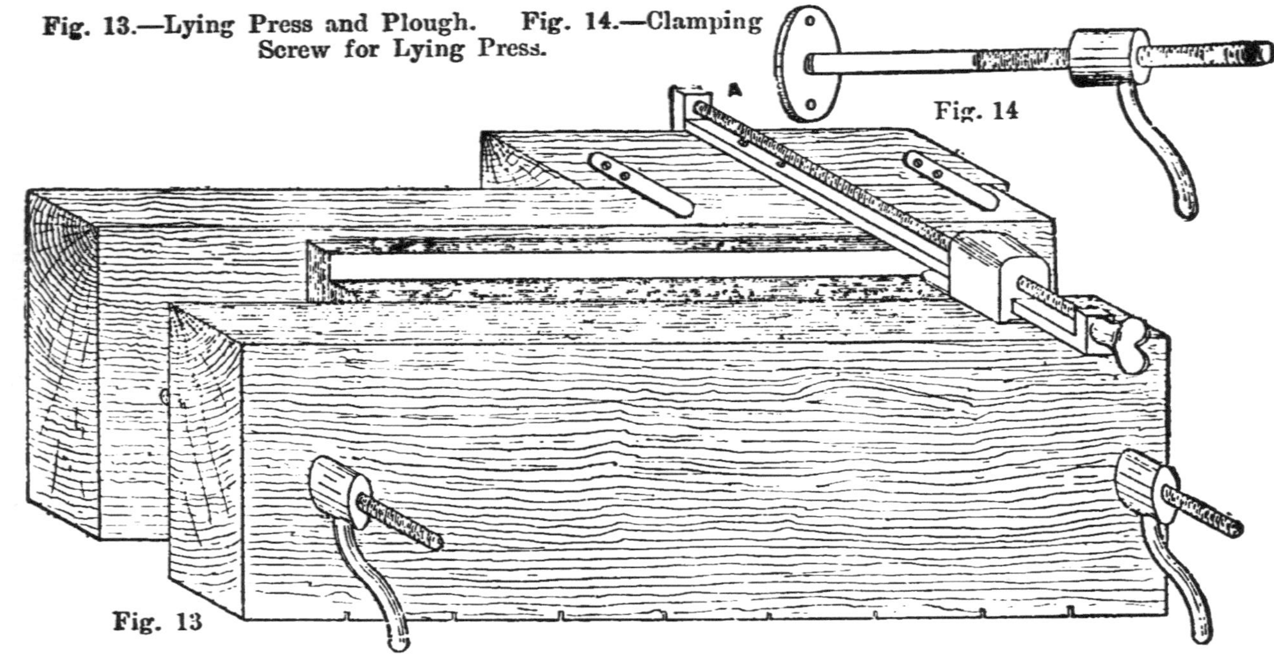

Fig. 13.—Lying Press and Plough. Fig. 14.—Clamping Screw for Lying Press.

and forwards, and also from turning round while the press is in use. Now put on the front and screw the boards together with the handles. Turn the press over so as to have the edges that are level uppermost, and then with a broad-set saw cut notches about $\frac{1}{4}$ in. deep at intervals of about 2 in. apart right across the two boards, as shown at the bottom of Fig. 13. The lying press itself is complete, but for convenience is attached to a support which serves as a guide to keep the books perfectly level while arranging them for binding. To make the support, procure a piece of board about $\frac{3}{4}$ in. thick and 14 in. by 12. in., and a piece of 1-in. board 14 in. by 8 in., and screw them together at right angles by their longer edges. The press is supported on the larger piece, the 14-in. by 8-in. piece standing upright on edge. On top of the back board of the press is laid a piece of wood 5 in. by 14 in. by $1\frac{1}{2}$ in., and this is screwed to the upright back of the support to form a continuation of the back board of the press.

It has been remarked that a press must have a good support if required to work with convenience. So many things are done with this appliance—pressing, cutting, backing, screwing-out, screwing-in, etc.—that as it is not very heavy it is always shifting on the table or bench, and thus causing trouble. To remedy all these inconveniences, one method is to make a combined press and box. In a box from 2 ft. 6 in. to 3 ft. long, 2 ft. wide, and 2 ft. deep, fix two pieces of beech wood (5 in. by 4 in.) A and B (Fig. 15, p. 20) of the same length as the inside measurement of box. The wood must be planed straight and squared up; bore holes for the screws C, say $1\frac{1}{4}$ in. diameter. Inside the box, on ends, nail two bars of wood D (as shown by dotted lines in Fig. 15), 5 in. from top, so that the front and back pieces of the press, when placed on them, will come level with the top of the box. Obtain iron screws and nuts to fit, say 1 in. or 1¼ in. diameter, of the shape shown at c, and on the nuts have tails with two holes for screw-nails to fasten into the press bar, cutting a hole in the wood so that the nut may be inserted flat.

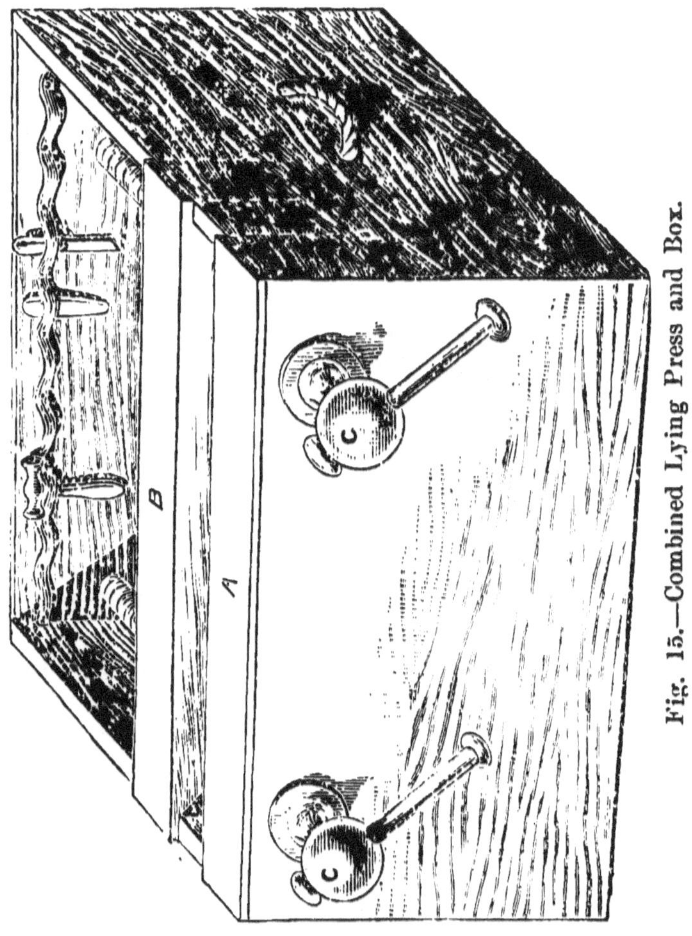

Fig. 15.—Combined Lying Press and Box.

The plough is the implement by which ordinarily the edges of well-bound books are cut. The plough consists of a couple of wooden cheeks, which can be brought together or drawn apart by rotating the handle and screw. To the bottom of the right cheek is fixed a plough knife, which is a blade of well-tempered steel secured to the under surface of the right-hand cheek of the plough by a screwed bolt and nut. Fig. 12 shows the plough as it lies ready for use in the cutting press. The book is carefully screwed up in the press, and the edges of the book are cut by sliding the plough forwards and backwards. The guiding groove on the plough is on the left-hand side of the press. On the right-hand side of the plough is a handle that turns the screw by which the knife is pushed laterally across the edges of the book every time the plough is thrust forward. Plough knifes are shown at A and B, Fig. 12, p. 17.

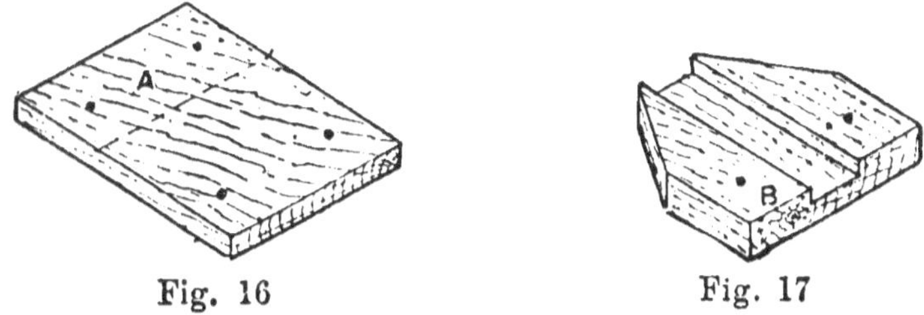

Fig. 16   Fig. 17

Figs. 16 and 17.—Details of Home-made Plough

Home-made ploughs are serviceable tools, and can be constructed from simple material, such as a chisel, some pieces of wood, and a few screws. Knock off the handle from an ordinary $\frac{1}{2}$-in. chisel having a " shoulder " near the haft, and replace it with a cork ; cut to the shape of Fig. 16 a piece of thin wood (say $\frac{1}{4}$ in. thick) $2\frac{1}{2}$ in. in breadth, its length depending on the length of the chisel. Place the chisel on the wood so that the cutting end overhangs about $1\frac{5}{8}$ in. ; at the other end mark where the shoulder of the chisel touches the wood, and cut across just above the mark so that the shoulder falls over the edge and allows the chisel to lie flat on the wood. Cut another piece of wood thicker than the last (of full $\frac{1}{2}$-in. stuff) to the shape of Fig. 17.

This will be, say, 2½ in. in breadth, 1¼ in. along its parallel sides, and 2½ in. in extreme length. Cut a groove down the middle as wide as the widest part of the chisel and as deep generally as the chisel is thick, but a little deeper than this towards the end

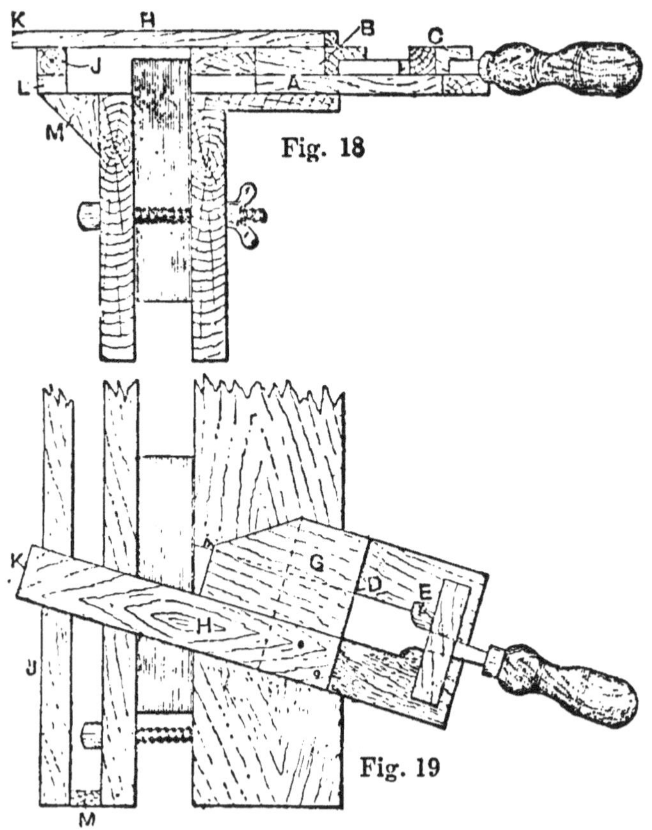

Fig. 18.—Elevation of Home-made Plough.   Fig. 19.—Plan of Home-made Plough.

B. Put the second piece of wood, groove downwards, on the first one so that the square end B of Fig. 17 rests upon the portion marked A of Fig. 16, allowing the pointed end to overhang. Screw the two pieces together from underneath, taking care to countersink the screw-heads. In the tunnel thus formed insert the chisel with its *bevelled edge upwards,* as it must always be when in use, and see that it has a rather loose fit. If it is all right, the cutting edge will project about $\frac{3}{8}$ in. at one end, and the shoulder will just fall over the edge at the other end. In a piece of wood c (Fig. 18), measuring, say, 2 in. by $\frac{1}{2}$ in. by $\frac{1}{2}$ in., make a groove of the same width as before, but a trifle deeper than the groove is at B (Fig. 17). Screw this last piece to the foundation A (Fig. 18) so that the groove en-

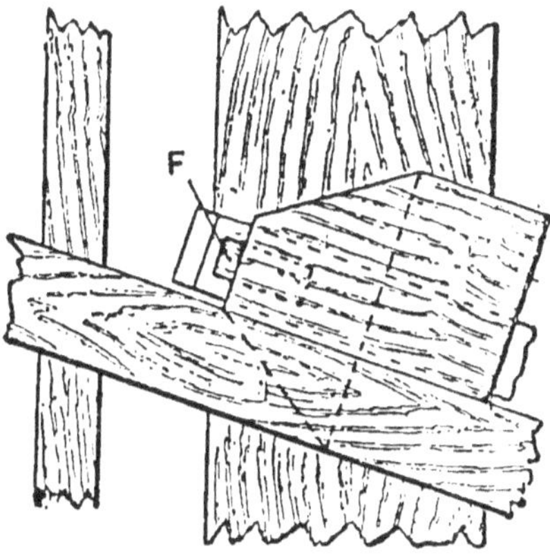

Fig. 20.—Wedges and Chisel of Home-made Plough.

closes the chisel just below the shoulder when the chisel is lying in the position above described. Insert a little wedge above the chisel beneath G (Fig. 19) so that the blade is prevented from moving up and down; also put in wedges at D and E, and one above the chisel at F (see Fig. 20). The whole will then be perfectly rigid, and the chisel will be firmly fixed in position, though, by taking out the wedges, it can be withdrawn readily for the purpose of sharpening it. Being thus easily removable, it is as useful as ever for other purposes than cutting book edges.

The body of the plough is now complete. It is,

of course, intended to be pushed to and fro upon the right cheek of the press; but the tool, as it stands, will not cut straight through so as to leave a nice flat surface, but will rise until it has made a "hog's-back." To prevent this, provide a bar of wood H (Figs. 18 and 19), which should be fixed at one end to the top G of the plough, and should rest at the other end on a guide-rail J fixed to the top face of the left cheek of the press. The bar should be rigid, say of $\frac{1}{2}$-in. stuff about 8 in. long, and be fixed to the plough with two screws. The top surface of the rail must be level with the top face of B (see Fig. 18); the easiest way to effect this will be to make the rail J of the same stuff as Fig. 17, and let it stand at each end on feet L (Fig. 18), made of the same stuff as Fig. 16. The bar will then lie quite horizontal across the press. Notice, too, that the rail J should be set back 1 in. or more from the inner edge of the left cheek, otherwise it will interfere with the "backing" operations.

In working, grasp the body of the plough with the right hand, and with the left keep the end K (Figs. 18 and 19) of the bar always touching the rail. When it is desired to work the plough outwards, set the detached end of bar K a little outwards so that the bar shall be at a slight angle, as shown in Fig. 19. Keep it at that angle, and move the plough from the near end of the book to the farther end, pressing the chisel edge quite lightly against the book. The first finger of the left hand, as it presses against the side of the rail, will regulate to a great extent the depth of the cut. If the woodwork has been properly executed, it will be possible to work the plough both backwards and forwards by simply alternating the left end of the bar; but if there is any unevenness in the woodwork, the chisel edge will not travel both ways in identically the same line, but will make two separate cuts. In such a case the plough must be worked one way only—it will not matter which. The edge of the chisel, as used in this case, should act with a drawing cut like that of a knife, and not with a thrusting cut like that of a chisel as ordinarily used. Be careful, therefore, not to incline the bar more than is shown in the illustration.

It is of the greatest importance that the chisel edge should be kept very sharp and in good shape by means of grindstone and oilstone. It is also important that the book edges be screwed up tight in the press. If the press used is an amateur contrivance of 1-in. stuff worked with screw bolts, as shown by Figs. 18 and 19, fix a little platform for the plough to run along upon the top of the right press cheek, and support the rail on brackets M

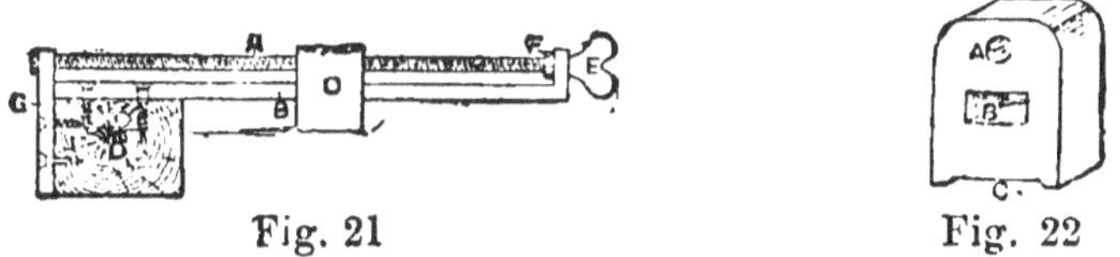

Fig. 21   Fig. 22

Fig. 21.—Plough.   Fig. 22.—Sliding Block for Plough.

fixed to the outer side of the left cheek. A cutting board of some sort (not shown) must be placed against the left side of the book.

The plough shown by Fig. 21 is for use with the lying press shown by Fig. 13, p. 18. It has a screw A made by threading from one end to the other a piece of iron wire about No. 4 B.W.G., 8 in. long. Fix a washer at F with a bit of solder, leaving enough of the wire projecting beyond it to pass through the hole in the flat bar and for a thumb-bolt E to screw on. The wing-nut can be made of brass, with a rounded neck and flat wings. Drill and tap it to screw tightly on to the wire, and leave it before fixing it on while the bar B is made. Procure 8 in. of $\frac{1}{4}$-in. by $\frac{1}{2}$ in. fiat iron, and bend about $\frac{3}{4}$-in. up at one end, as shown in the sketch. File it up perfectly true and smooth all over, and then drill a hole at F for the screw to pass through easily, and drill and countersink two holes at the other end for the heads of two $1\frac{1}{2}$-in. screws to drop in. C (Fig. 21) is the sliding block, and D is an end view of the runner block. It is important that the sliding block (Fig. 22, p. 25) be accurate. Get a block of brass 1 in. by 1 in. by $1\frac{1}{4}$ in., carefully square it up, and then round the top corners a little, as illustrated. Cut an oblong hole $\frac{1}{2}$ in. by $\frac{1}{4}$ in. at B for the bar B (Fig. 21) to pass through. If two holes (not quite $\frac{1}{4}$ in. in diameter) are drilled through side by side, it will be easy, with a small chisel and file, to cut the hole to the desired shape. See that it fits the bar well—not loosely—and then drill and tap a hole at A the same size as the screw already made. If the block is slid along the bar till it is against the bit that is turned up, the proper position for the hole will at once be found by passing a needle through the hole already in the bar and marking a corresponding circle on the block C. If any doubt exists about getting these holes through accurately, mark the block on both sides, and drill also from both sides till the holes meet in the middle. Next cut the slot C $\frac{1}{16}$ in. deep and $\frac{3}{4}$ in. wide, dovetailed to fit the bar B. Bevel a bit of good steel, $\frac{3}{4}$ in. broad and $\frac{1}{16}$ in. thick, to fit in the block tightly, and, while it is in, drill and tap a hole through it, and also into the block, so that a small screw may be inserted to keep it from slipping out when it is in use. Make a small screw for the purpose just stated, and then proceed to finish the knife (Fig. 23). Be careful, when the screw is put into its place, that it does not project above the surface of the knife, or it will tear the edges of the book as it passes to and fro when in use. The knife is now rounded at the end, as seen in Fig. 23, and then bevelled off to the shape shown. Fig. 23 represents it as it would appear if looked at from underneath.

When it has been nicely tempered, it may be fixed
in its place in the block. A piece of flat iron, 2¼ in.
long and about ½ in. broad, forms a support for
the end of the long screw. This is shown at G
(Fig. 21). Near the top drill a hole in which the
screw A revolves, and make two holes for the screws
which fix it in its place, and the various parts of
the cutter are ready to be put together. Slide the
block C on to the bar B and the long screw A, and
fix the wing-nut on the end by screwing it on
tightly, and then secure it by passing a small screw
through the neck into the screw A. Now fix the

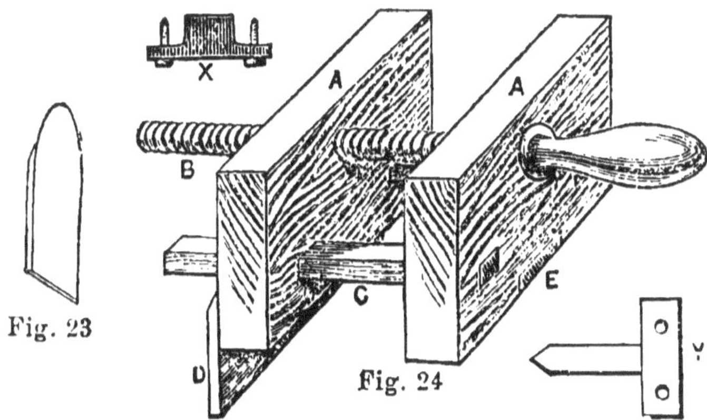

Fig. 23. —Plough Knife.   Fig. 24.—Plough.

bar on a piece of 2-in. by 1½-in. wood about 8 in.
long and screw on the guide-plate G. It will be
advisable to fix on two pieces of metal, as in Fig.
13 (p. 18), to keep the cutter from twisting. This
tool will cut through any book as perfectly as one
costing a hundred times as much.

Still another kind of plough, resembling one previously described, however, is illustrated by Fig.
24. To make it, obtain two pieces of seasoned
beech for the sides A, about 8 in. long by 4 in. deep,
and 1¼ in. or 1½ in. thick; also obtain a ¾-in. iron
screw and nut with tail, to insert in the side

opposite to the handle. By using a wooden screw, a hole could be tapped in the side piece, and the trouble of inserting the iron nut would be saved. Two guides c, say 10 inches long and 1 in. square, are fixed in the handle side, say 1½ in. from the bottom: they slide through square holes. A notch is made to receive the cutting knife, as shown at E, so that when put on with two screw nails the knife is flat with the wood, as will be seen. To ensure movement in both directions, a hole is bored through the screw spindle for the pin and washer. The side now is all of one piece, and will move out or in as required. It remains to put a slip of wood or iron on the other side, so that it may hold on to the press bar B while working the plough backwards and forwards to cut the edge held in the press. This hardwood slip is shown at D. x (Fig. 24) is the iron which carries the knife, the shape of which is indicated by Y.

The guillotine is another kind of cutting machine for trimming the edges of books. The name of the machine sufficiently explains for the present purpose its construction and the manner of using it. It is expensive, and is used for cloth books.

The tub is the stand on which the lying press is supported. The sides of the tub are often boarded up for some distance from the floor, to contain the shavings cut from the book edges. A large, open rectangular packing case makes a good tub.

A pair of large stout shears (similar to those employed by tinsmiths), one handle of which is held in the press, the other being worked by the binder, is desirable when much cutting up of millboards for book covers has to be done, though a sharp knife, like that used by shoemakers, will answer the purpose. It is, of course, obvious that a smooth, hard bed for cutting on must be provided, and, if a knife is used, a steel straightedge or T-square is required as a guide for the knife. A grindstone and oilstone are very economical additions, for all cutting tools must be kept sharp.

The holing machine is used for perforating the covers of books. These holes are intended for the reception of the ends of the bands or cords by which the book is attached to its covers; but a bradawl or a bodkin or a small punch will answer the purpose of a holing machine. A tenon saw is required for making the "kerfs," which are grooves or cuts made across the back of a book to hold the bands or cords upon which the sheets of the book are sewn. These cuts are made when the book is screwed up tightly in the lying press.

Backing boards are of very hard wood, as they have to resist considerable strain, and are made in pairs, of the usual book sizes. The purpose for which backing boards are used, and the shape of the boards (the bevels being somewhat exaggerated for the sake of clearness), will be seen on reference to Figs. 35 and 36, pp. 49 and 51. Cutting boards, as their name implies, are placed on each side of the book when its edges are cut, and they are not so thick as backing boards. Though both backing boards and cutting boards can be made by an amateur, he is advised to purchase a pair of backing boards to serve as a pattern for those he may afterwards make.

Sundry small tools include one or two pairs of scissors, a sharp-pointed knife for squaring plates— that is, single-leaf illustrations—large sewing needles, a small wooden tub for thick paste and an earthenware vessel for thin paste, a large glue-pot for thin glue and a smaller pot for thick glue, with brushes for applying both paste and glue, sprinkle pot (any large stoneware vessel or gallipot will do), a sprinkle-brush, which must be a well-made brush with a stout wrought-iron ferrule (not a bit of common hoop iron, but a ferrule made by a smith), an agate burnisher, that known as a dog's tooth being

the most useful, a backing hammer, a small round
marble slab and paring knife, one or two bent
pointed folding-sticks, and a pair of iron compasses.
Many of these tools, or such as may very well be
substituted for them, are already possessed by the
majority of amateur workers. Other tools may be
constructed, or may be purchased second-hand of
printers' brokers. An ingenious amateur will con-
trive many mechanical aids for facilitating his work
as soon as he understands the purpose to be ac-
complished. An expensive plant, therefore, is not
absolutely necessary to enable anyone to begin

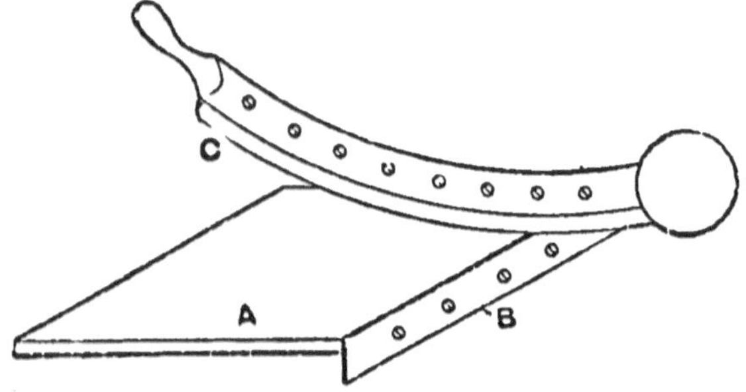

Fig. 25.—Strawboard Cutter.

bookbinding. It is, however, obvious that proper
tools and machines lessen labour and save time.

It is possible that particulars of a machine for
cutting strawboard, cardboard, etc., may be useful.
The appliance shown by Fig. 25 consists of a wood
or iron table A resting on a framework and four legs.
On the table are gauges, which can be so adjusted
that the operator can cut the boards to any size required. Close to the edge of the table is a clamp
to hold the boards in position while being cut. This
clamp is worked by the foot, a treadle being provided at the bottom of the legs, near the floor. The
boards are cut between two knives, one, B, being
screwed flush to the edge of the table, and the
other, C, being movable and screwed to the lever.

The edges of the knives are bevelled like scissor blades; in fact, the machine is simply a large pair of scissors. A balance weight at the end of the movable arm carries the knife and keeps it in position. Both knives should be made of steel, and in tempering them avoid getting them too hard, or they will be liable to chip. Fig. 26 represents the gauge A on top of the table. This gauge is simply an L-shaped piece of metal; the shorter branch of the L is bent to lie close to the edge of the table. A slot almost the entire length of the gauge is cut in the latter. A thumbscrew screws into the edge of the table and fastens the gauge in position. The

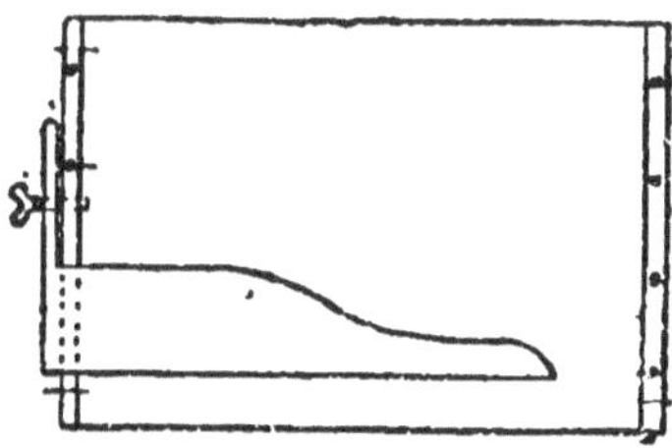

Fig. 26.—Gauge of Strawboard Cutter.

other portion of the gauge lies flat on the table. The clamp is a light casting shaped like Fig. 27, p. 32. It is fitted to the table close up to the knife B (Fig. 25). A short rod is fixed at one end of the clamp and a longer rod at the other end, ending in a stirrup for the foot. These rods are fitted with springs which raise the clamp and hold it up until the foot is placed in the stirrup. A little pressure on the stirrup brings down the clamp and holds the board while it is being cut. The stirrup should reach almost to the floor for convenience of working. The side of the table and the front of the gauge must be a perfect right angle, otherwise difficulty will be experienced in cutting the boards straight. Strips of iron, not quite $\frac{1}{8}$ in. thick and perfectly straight on the inner edges, are screwed

to the top of the table as shown. The strawboard
is placed against these strips and the gauge when

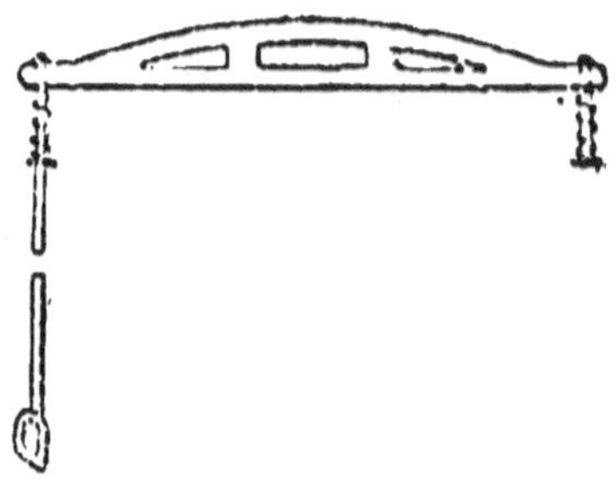

Fig. 27.—Clamp of Strawboard Cutter.

cutting, the clamp is applied, and the knife brought
down forcibly. Such a machine is in general use
amongst bookbinders, paper-box makers, etc.

Bookbinders use large quantities of glue in their
work, and doubtless much time would be saved by
employing some such preparation as " Gloophlex," an
elastic glue, guaranteed by the makers to be strong
and reliable. As bought, it has the smell and appearance of consistent glue-jelly, and the only preparation
needed is to melt it by heating it on a water bath, and
then add boiling water according to requirements.

CHAPTER II.

FOLDING PRINTED BOOK SHEETS.

THE first operation in bookbinding is folding the printed sheets, and it requires great care if the book is to have a good appearance when bound. It is usual for printers to leave more margin to the outsides of the sheet, so that when the sheets have been folded the margin will be broader at the fore-edge and tail than at the head and back. The head and back are always at the fold, the tail and fore-edge being towards the outside of the sheet. If the paper presents any little difference in size, the, two latter edges being cut first in the process of binding, the difference will then be taken off, and the margin will be the same all round.

The plan adopted is to fold to the pages of print, and not to the edge of the paper, for the least variation in the size of the sheet would result in a spoiled book.

Papers are made in various sizes, and are known by the following terms : Imperial (30 in. by 22 in.), royal (25 in. by 20 in.), demy ($22\frac{1}{2}$ in. by $17\frac{1}{2}$ in.), crown (20 in. by 15 in.), foolscap (17 in. by $13\frac{1}{2}$ in.), and pott (15 in. by $12\frac{1}{2}$ in.) ; and the sizes of books are denominated according to the number of leaves into which the sheet is folded. The ordinary sizes are folio, 4to, 8vo, 12mo, 16mo, 24mo, and 32mo. A sheet, when folded, has twice as many pages as leaves, for the obvious reason that it is printed on both sides. In speaking of the size of *The Quiver*, for example, it is said to be royal octavo (8vo), because the sheet has been folded to one-eighth its original size, and has sixteen pages. The octavo is

the most general size of a book, and the type matter
is so imposed that, when the sheet is folded, the
sixteen pages will follow consecutively.

In the early days of printing only a few pages
could be printed at one operation. Now, however,
the number of pages that can be printed on one
sheet of paper is only limited by the size of the
printing machine. But, as a matter of convenience,
the sheets the binder has to deal with usually consist of 4, 8, 16, 32, 64, or 128 pages, the number of
pages that are folded into one sheet depending on
the price at which the book is to be sold. In the
best work, the sheets do not contain more than
sixteen pages—that is, eight pages on each side
of a sheet of paper; and each sixteen pages is
called a section or sheet. At the bottom of one of
the pages (the first numerically) of each sheet is
printed a letter or figure, known as the signature ;
this is the guide when folding, and, as the letters
or figures follow each other consecutively, the placing of the sheets in their proper order when sewing
them is thus ensured. Thus, when the sheets in a
work each consist of sixteen pages, the signatures
will be found at the foot of pp. 1, 17, 33, 49, etc.
The manner of folding is as follows : A printed sheet
(say, pp. 1 to 16) is laid on a table in front of the
operator, that side of the sheet containing p. 1 (the
signature side) lying in contact with the table.
Page 2 backs p. 1, and p. 2 should be the corner
page close to the operator's left-hand (see Fig. 28).
The corner page at the folder's right-hand is p. 3.
The object to be obtained is to fold the sheet over
in such a way as to place the figure 3 exactly on the
top of the figure 2. If this is properly done, the
printed lines on p. 3 will lie exactly on the printed
lines on p. 2, line for line, and when the book is
bound the white margins round the print on each
page will all be of the same relative widths, the
front and the bottom margins being always wider

than the top and the inside margins. The result of the first fold is shown by Fig. 29. The second fold brings pp. 5 and 12 over on to pp. 4 and 13; the result of this fold is shown by Fig. 30. The third fold brings p. 9 on to p. 8, the folded sheet is turned over, and the result seen by Fig. 31. The first page is p. 1, containing the signature, in this case the letter A, and the last page of the sheet is p. 16. All folding operations follow this general plan of doubling over the sheet for each fold; to this rule there are, of course, a few exceptions, but these are easily recognised. Before beginning to fold, the folder should ascertain how many pages

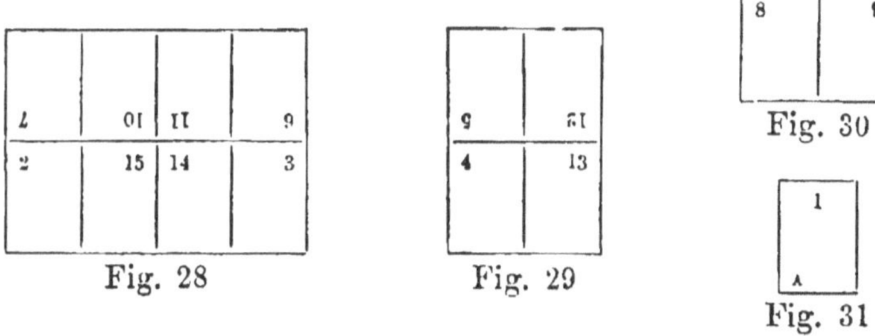

Fig. 28.—Printed Book Sheet.   Fig. 29.—Printed Sheet, First Fold.   Fig. 30.—Printed Sheet, Second Fold. Fig. 31.—Printed Sheet, Third Fold.

are contained in a section. To every section belongs a distinguishing signature or letter, and all the pages coming between the first page of, say, signature A and the first page of signature B belong to signature A. Thus it may happen that signature A consists of thirty-two pages; but in order to ensure better folding, the thirty-two pages are printed so as to fold in two sections, one of which is inserted in the centre of the other. The pages and signatures are then arranged as follows: The outer sheet contains pp. 1 (signature A) to 8 and pp. 25 to 32; the inner sheet, called the inset, contains pp. 9 (signature A*) to 24. The sheet and its inset are folded independently of each other in the manner already described, and when the inset is inserted p. 9 follows p. 8, and p. 25 follows p. 24. This is the general rule applicable to all insets of this character. Exceptions to this rule may, of course, occur, but these exceptions would probably be caused by the limited plant of the printer who produced the book. A sheet may consist of several insets, but the signatures would follow the rule already stated. The worker must be always on the look-out for things of this kind. Figures as well as letters are used as signature marks; where letters are used, the first sheet of the book (excluding the title and contents) sometimes begins with B instead of A, and the letters J and V are not used in all cases. The folder is held in the right hand, and is used for smoothing the folds, etc. Creasing and puckering of the folds must be guarded against; these mishaps readily occur if the folder is not properly used.

In order the better to describe the further stages of binding, let it be supposed that the operator is dealing with one book consisting of nineteen sections, each section, except the title sheet, which contains eight pages only, consisting of sixteen pages. This will give a total of 288 pages of text and eight pages of introductory matter, consisting of title page, preface, and contents. The signatures of the sheets, omitting the letter J, will run from B to T, and the title sheet will not contain a signature. The sheets must be placed in their proper order, and the folded edges, which will be the heads and the backs of the sections, brought level by knocking them up on the table. The embryo book may now be placed in the press between a couple of boards, and subjected to pressure in order that the sheets may lie closely together.

In large establishments, folding is done by machinery, without which it would be impossible for the enormous quantities of work to be turned out. There are a great many machines in the market, and it would be difficult to say which is best. Nearly all bookbinders' engineers manufacture folding machines, and some are manufactured with special features to suit certain requirements. Cundall's is a very good machine, which does its work well without any special attention, and will do two, three, or four folds. It has a nice tidy delivery, and is easily set from one size to another. Its speed is close on 1,700 per hour, so that, with a very ordinary feeder, it will fold 1,500 sheets per hour. The Salmon machine acts much on the same principle. The name of Martini is well known in England in connection with the Martini-Henry rifle, but on the Continent his name is still more famous for the invention of the single and duplex folding machine; and a wonderful machine it is, folding sheets of paper by means of a series of cross metal knives, folding true to register, and delivering in a trough already knocked up. Binders in this country were slow in adopting this class of machine. With the tape machine there always is a large number of re-folds at the end of the day's work, and there is the risk of a tape breaking at an awkward moment. Both of these evils are entirely obviated by the Martini folders, for there is not an inch of moving tape used to carry the sheet from fold to fold. Two girls feed the machine; they stand each with a pile of sheets below her hand, at the ends of the machine, feeding them one by one to the points or gauges. The sheet is carried immediately to the centre of the table, first from one side, then from the other, the knife going up and down away from where the girls are standing, causing the sheet to disappear. Such a machine can get through an enormous quantity of work.

CHAPTER III.

BEATING AND SEWING.

IT has already been suggested (see p. 11) that beating is now confined almost wholly to small offices, although in special cases it may be adopted even when a rolling machine is generally used. Beating is, however, the cheapest process for the amateur. The object of beating is to make the leaves of a book lie close together, so that the volume when bound may be as solid as though it were one single block. Mere pressing alone will not do this. In beating, the bookbinder stands before the beating slab, holding in his left hand a bundle of as many sections of the book as he deems advisable to operate upon at once, say, from five up to ten or fifteen, according to the thickness of the paper. The bundle of sheets is beaten for some time with the hammer, which has already been described. The proper use of the beating hammer requires so much manual dexterity that it is advisable to practise beating with a few folded sheets of blank paper. The handle is grasped with the right hand, with the big knuckles downward and the wrist curved. The wrist and hand are then slightly twisted so as to give the face of the hammer an upward turn that almost permits the operator to see the face of the hammer. Then, by a downward turn, the hammer is allowed to descend on the work. The blow must be given with very little more force than is furnished by the weight of the hammer. The hammer must not by any chance fall edgewise on the sheets; if it does, many leaves will be cut through, and the work spoilt. The bundle of sheets must be constantly shifted and evenly struck all over, and a sheet of stiff, smooth paper, placed at the top and bottom of the bundle, will keep the sheets clean. The solidity of a bound book depends on the amount of beating or rolling it receives.

If it is necessary to bind very recently printed sheets, they must not be beaten or rolled; nor should this be done if the ink is so wet as to smear, or the ink will set off, as it is technically termed; that is, the printing on each page will be partly transferred to the facing page, and both pages will be somewhat illegible. The sheets of a new work should, before they are folded, be hung on lines in a dry, well-ventilated room till the ink is thoroughly dry. Test the sheets by placing a piece of white paper on a printed page; rub the paper hard with a folder or the finger nail, and if there is then no sign of setting off, the sheets may safely be beaten or rolled.

Many bookbinders who possess a rolling machine will probably roll an amateur's work at a very small cost. There are also houses that do rolling for the trade. Beating, however, will answer very well. Indeed, very old books should on no account be rolled; the paper on which they are printed being uneven in thickness, and the actual printing having been done under varying degrees of pressure, careful beating must take the place of rolling, or the work will be spoilt. After the sheets of a book have been beaten a few at a time, all the sheets of the volume should be beaten together and then placed once more for a short time in the standing press.

Cutting with a saw several kerfs or channels across the back of the book is the next operation, and this is to allow of sewing. In order to do this, the book (either one or many) is screwed up in the lying press, either between pressing boards or backing boards, which are placed slightly below the level of the back to allow the cut to be made. If a lying press is not available, an ordinary carpenter's bench will answer the purpose. The back of the book is, according to its size, now divided into a certain number of spaces, mostly equal; but owing to a common optical illusion, in order that all the spaces shall appear to be of the same size, the bottom space must be about $\frac{1}{2}$ in. larger than the others. At the points of division lines are drawn across the back of the book, and these lines mark the bands or cords on which the book is to be sewn, through, for ornamental purposes, books are often marked up for, say, five bands and only sewn on three, the dummy bands being fastened on when the book receives its cover. In flexible work the back is not sawn in except for the kettle stitch or catching stitch, the bands or cords being outside the sheet, the thread being sewn around them. In the other kind, the back is sawn across at the places marked, the cut for the kettle stitch being very shallow, only deep enough, in fact, to take a chain stitch of single thread. Octavos are generally sawn for five bands; larger or smaller books have more or fewer bands, according to size, because in the larger books the number of leaves in a section are few, and the thread has less substance to hold on to than in the smaller books.

The twine or string used for the bands varies in size according to the size of the book; it is named after it, and is sold by that name. In the case of large books, where the cord is thick, a plan that has been successfully adopted is to use two pieces of thin cord instead of one thick piece. This method has much to recommend it.

The cuts, which are made with a tenon saw, should be perfectly level, should not be deeper on one side than on the other, and should be just large enough to receive and hide the cord. If the saw has a thin blade. it should be inclined just a little alternately to the right and to the left, so as to widen the bottom of the kerf. Fig. 32 shows the saw kerfs.

Sewing books is very simple, but somewhat

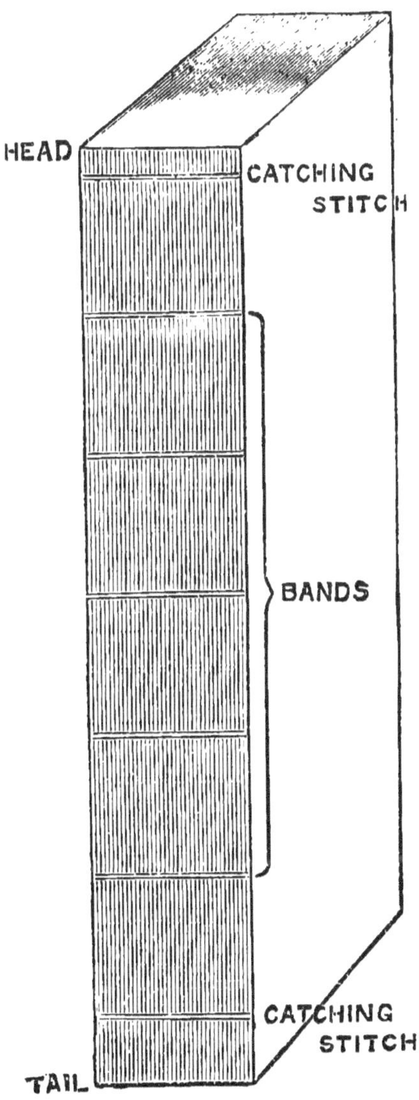

Fig. 32.—Saw Kerfs in Back of Book.

difficult to describe clearly. The amateur should endeavour to obtain some practical instruction in the art. The sewing press and keys are illustrated by Figs. 4 to 10, pp. 13 to 16; the other requisites are cord for the bands, thread, needles, and a couple of folding-sticks. The cross-bar of the press having been screwed up to the proper height, the required number of loops of string are fastened round it. To each of the loops a length of cord is attached by a bow knot that can readily be untied, and the other end of the cord then is wound round a key, which is pushed lengthwise through a long slot in the front of the bed of the sewing press, and then turned crosswise to it below, so as to remain in that position. The bands are adjusted to correspond with the saw kerfs in the back of the book, and the cross-bar of the sewing press is screwed up by turning the wooden nuts on each screw until the bands are taut. The press is placed on the edge of a bench of suitable height, and the sewer sits before it in such a position that the left arm rests on the bed of the press (see Fig. 33). Bookbinders' thread, which must be of good quality, is supplied by the dealers in bookbinders' materials, as are also the needles. If only one book is to be sewn it will be found convenient to raise it from the bed of the press by placing another book under it. It is, of course, a saving of time in the preparation of the work to sew at one sitting as many books as the press will hold. The first and the last sections of a book should be overcast, this being generally done with fine cotton. The sewer lifts the first section of the book from the pile of sawn sheets on the bench. This, which will be the title sheet (consisting of the title page and contents), is placed face downward on the bed of the press so that the several cords enter their respective saw channels. The head of the book is at the sewer's right hand. The needle is passed into the saw cut for the kettle stitch at the tail of the book, then passed along the middle of the section and out at the near side of the first cord. The needle next enters on the farther side of the cord, passes along the middle of the section to the centre cord, and out on the near side. The needle again enters on the farther side of this cord, passes along the middle of the section to the third or top band, and is brought out on the near side. The needle is then inserted on

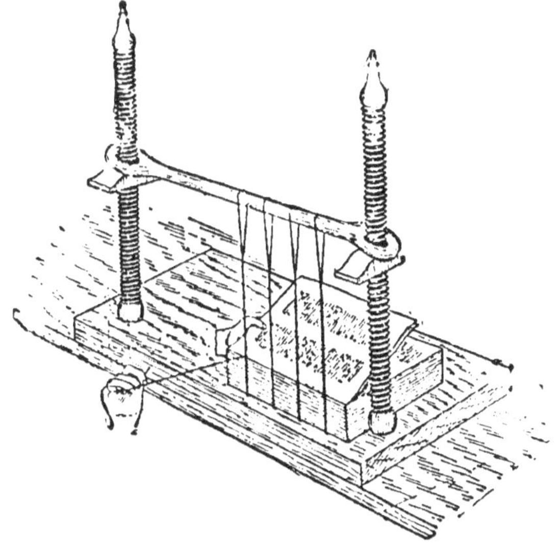

Fig. 33.—Sewing Book.

the farther side of this cord, passes along the middle of the section, and comes out at the side of the kerf made for the top kettle stitch. The thread now runs along the centre of the section from kettle stitch to kettle stitch, except where the cords occur, where it passes round the outside of them. It is obvious that by this process the sheet is securely attached to the bands or cords. The thread is now drawn tight and smooth, about 1 in. of the end being left protruding from the lower kettle stitch. The second sheet of the book (which will be signature B if the first section had a signature, otherwise it will be signature A) is laid face downward upon the first sheet. The needle is inserted at the top kettle stitch, and the sewing is done in the same way as with the first sheet, except that the needle travels towards instead of from the sewer. Having brought the needle out of the opening for the lower kettle stitch and pulled the thread tightly along the section, the slack of the thread is firmly knotted to the end thread left hanging from the kettle stitch, the knot being made twice for greater security. The remainder of the sheets will be sewn "two on," except the last two sheets, which are sewn on like the first two sheets. In sewing two on, the sheet C is laid on the two sheets already sewn, and the thread, which has not been detached from A and B, is passed from the tail kettle stitch of C to the first band along the centre of the section. A folder is then put in the middle of the section to mark the place. Section D is then laid on C and is sewn from the farther side of the first band to the near side of the third one ; then section C, the middle of which is easily found by the folder, is sewn along from the third band to the head kettle stitch, two sections being thus secured by a single passage of the needle from tail to head, or *vice versâ.* These two sheets are secured at the head or the tail by making a kettle stitch. This is effected by passing the needle under the section already sewn, up through the loop thus formed by the thread, and then upwards until the knot is drawn tight, taking care that the stitch is kept in the saw mark cut for it, and that it does not tear the back of the section. When the needleful of thread is finished, it must not be fastened off on the book, but the second needleful must be knotted to the first so that the book is sewn with one length of thread.

Fig. 34 may help to explain a method of sewing "two on." A, B, and C represent the first three sheets; 1, 2, 3, 4, and 5 the saw-marks and the position of the bands. The small letters, if taken in alphabetical order, will show the outs and ins of the needle. Thus in at a, A, out at b, in at c,

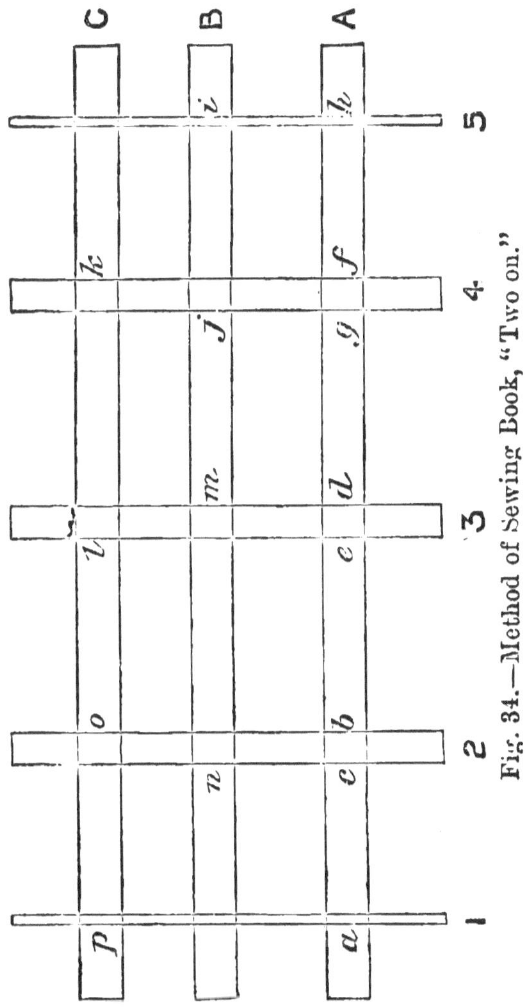

Fig. 34.—Method of Sewing Book, "Two on."

out at d, and so on until h is reached; the needle will be at the outside of the first sheet or A, which will have been sewn all the way up. Now in at i, in the second sheet or B; out at j, B; in at k, c;

out at *l*, c; in at *m*, B; out at *n*, B; in at *o*, c; out at *p*, c: and fasten. The diagram has little of the appearance of a book on the bench, its purpose being to show intricate matter plainly and simply.

The method of sewing just described is that which is used for non-flexible work—that is, for books in which the back of the cover is not glued to the backs of the sheets. In non-flexible work, when the book is opened the back of the cover forms an arch, leaving a space between it and the back of the book, but in flexible work the back of the book adheres to the cover. For flexible work the back is marked up, but is not sawn in, the cord or band being laid on the back of the book and not embedded in the sheets. The marks for the kettle stitches are sawn slightly, as in the case of non-flexible work. In sewing, the needle is passed in at the right-hand kettle-stitch hole; the left hand inside the section takes the needle and thrusts it out of the left side of the mark for the first band, and with the right-hand the needle is taken and thrust in on the right-hand side of the same band, so that the band or cord is encircled with the thread. The same operation is repeated at each band, and the needle finally brought out at the left-hand kettle-stitch hole. The other sheets are sewn in the same manner.

It is hardly necessary to point out that in flexible work the cord on which the books are sewn will, if no corrective measures are adopted, be seen through the leather covering. When it is desirable that the cords should not be seen, the spaces between the cords are levelled up with paper so that the back presents a smooth appearance. The levelling up is much easier when the sewing is done with strong tape instead of cord.

When several books of the same size are to be bound, they are usually sewn in the one stack. The cords, which are kept sufficiently long for the purpose, are then drawn out between the volumes and cut off so as to leave about 1½ in. of cord projecting at each side of the back, a three-band book having thus half a dozen ends. A few experiments in sewing will very soon demonstrate the fact that the kettle stitches pull the head and tail of the book together, and the thread swells out the middle. Care must be taken, therefore, that the kettle stitches are not pulled together too tightly, and the swelling must be counteracted by frequently beating down the back with a heavy folding-stick. Attention must also be paid to the thickness of the thread used in sewing ; when the sections are thin, the thread must be thin.

Overcasting is used when a number of single leaves have to be bound into a book, the plan being as follows : Having ascertained that the pages follow each other in proper order, the book is knocked up carefully at the head and the back and placed in the lying press between two boards, the back projecting about ⅛ in. above the pressing boards. The back is roughed with a saw and sawn in, after which thin glue is brushed over the back, and the book is left to dry. When dry, the book is pulled apart in sections, each section consisting of eight or sixteen pages, according to the size and other characteristics of the work. Each section is then oversewn along the back, the thread being fastened off at each end—that is, at the head or foot of the page. This is known as overcasting ; after this the sections are hammered lightly to embed the thread. This operation must be performed carefully, or the thread will be cut. Then these sections are sewn in the ordinary way, like other books. The first and the last two sheets of a book generally are overcast to lessen the possibility of their being torn away, by the weight of the covers, from the other sheets.

CHAPTER IV.

ROUNDING, BACKING, AND COVER CUTTING.

AT the beginning and end of almost any book is a leaf of plain or plain and coloured paper popularly known as fly-leaves, but by the bookbinders called end papers. These end papers generally consist of a couple of stout leaves of coloured paper, one of which is pasted down to the cover of the book, and the other is a loose or fly-leaf; there may also be another fly-leaf of white paper. End papers are made by pasting sheets of white and coloured paper together. The coloured paper, which is specially made for this purpose, may be purchased with other bookbinding materials. The colour of the end paper is governed by the binding and by the colour of the edges of the book. The ends of the bands on which the book is sewn should be untwisted to separate the fibres by the aid of a bodkin and dull knife; an end paper is then affixed to each side of the book by pasting the back for a short way in. When the end papers are dry, the books should be knocked up perfectly square at the head and back by striking them on the cheek of the lying press, the backs being lightly but completely glued over. The glue should not be too thick, and the brush should be worked well in between the sections. The glue should then be allowed to set.

In the process of rounding the binder takes a book on which the glue has set, but is still plastic, and gently tapping each side of the back alternately with the backing hammer, aided by a drawing movement of the fingers of his left hand, which holds the book, upon the upper end paper, and a pressure

of his left thumb against the centre of the fore
edge, the binder deftly gives a slight regular curvature to the back. It is upon this curvature of the
back that the beauty of a well-bound book depends.
For example, it is the convexity of the back that
causes the agreeable concavity of the fore edge, and
adds much to the effect of the finishing or gilded
ornamentation of the volume.

Backing is the next operation, and is intended
to render the rounding of the back more regular,
and generally to consolidate it. The book, with a
backing board on each side, is placed in the lying

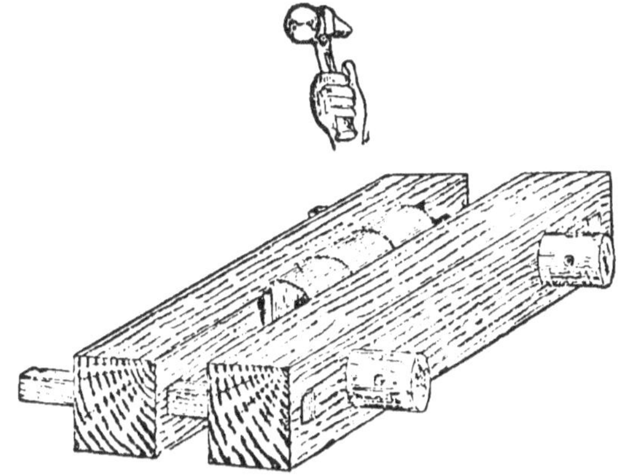

Fig. 35.—Method of Backing Book.

press, the highest part of the thick edge of the
board being within a short distance of the folded
edge of the end paper, just enough space being left
to form the joint or groove in which the board of
the cover works. The size of this groove depends
on the thickness of the cover board, which is, of
course, governed by the size of the book. The book,
with its boards, is carefully lowered into the press,
level with the upper surface of the cheeks, and
screwed up tightly. The book is then struck along
the back in order to spread it, and afterwards carefully hammered up and down each side with the

D

pene or face of the hammer (see Fig. 35) until the back has become solid, smooth, and well curved; it must also overhang the backing boards so as to form a well-defined groove on each side for the reception of the cover boards. At this stage of the operations the book should present in section the appearance shown in Fig. 36, where, however, for clearness, the grooves are somewhat exaggerated.

Cutting the boards or side covers of the book is the next step. The early bookbinders used wood for the side covers of their books, and the name has survived, though the material has changed. These wooden covers were often elaborately carved, and many specimens are still in existence. Deer's hide, silk, velvet, and, later on, leather, were afterwards used to cover up the wood. The material employed for ordinary leather binding at the present day is millboard.

The better qualities of millboard are made of sound old rope or cordage, and the boards are manufactured of different thicknesses, and are very tough. The darker the colour of the boards the better is the quality. Cheap millboards are adulterated with clay, which gives substance and weight to the boards, but does not impart tenacity. Millboards improve by keeping, and should not be used fresh from the mill. They are made in a variety of sizes and thicknesses, much in the way that printing papers are. What is termed "tip" is the thinnest variety, and is scarcely thicker than stout brown paper. This kind is useful for flexible bindings. The largest and stoutest millboards are principally employed by the portmanteau makers.

Strawboards are largely used for cheap work. As their name implies, they are made of straw, are very smooth and compact, but are so extremely brittle as to be useless for any purpose but cloth binding, cheap Bibles, and other common work. The amateur should not use them. The covers can be set out with the compasses, and marked off with a bodkin on a sheet of millboard of suitable thickness, and cut up into boards of the proper size, either with the millboard shears or with a sharp knife and straightedge.

For the better class of leather work, the required thickness of millboards is frequently made up by pasting two boards together, the inside board being thinner than the outer one. These made boards warp a little inwards, and this ensures a shapely cover that clings closely to the book. Single-board covers are, with the same purpose of slightly warping them, lined with paper. Lining should never be omitted. Unless the boards can be cut with shears or knife true and square at the edges, the

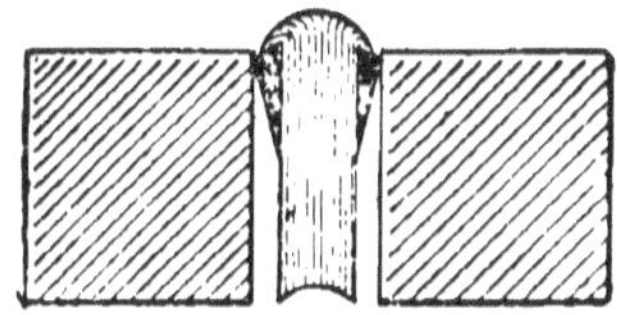

Fig. 36.—Book and Backing Boards in Lying Press.

boards should be cut with the plough. The amateur will probably find it cheaper at first, at any rate, to get his covers cut for him, and he should keep a pair of covers by him as a pattern. The covers of a book must be a little larger than the book itself after its edges are cut, and the squares, as these projecting portions of the cover are called, must be ascertained and allowed for by measuring with the compasses.

In lacing on or drawing in, a cut cover is placed in the correct position on each side of the book, and the positions of the bands are marked on it with the bodkin. Two holes slightly inclined towards each other for each band are made at the marked places, one from the outside, near the edge of the boards, and another from the inside, somewhat farther in. These holes can be made with a bodkin, piercer, or awl, with or without the aid of a hammer, or with the holing machine (see p. 29). The bands, which have been previously untwisted and fluffed out, then are pasted slightly, twirled up to a point, passed through the holes in the boards (those nearest the edge being taken first), and drawn tight. The protruding ends are then cut off tolerably close to the board and knocked down flat with the hammer and left to dry and set. The bands laced through the millboard are knocked down with the backing hammer on an iron plate (termed the knocking-down iron). The book is tapped along the sides of the back with the backing hammer in order to restore the proper curvature if it has been impaired at all during lacing in.

In the process of scratching up or raking, the books, with their backs protruding, are placed between pressing boards and stacked up in the standing press, which is screwed down tightly. After lightly pasting the back of each book, a " scratcher up " (Fig. 37) is drawn several times with some force down the back, care being taken, however, not to catch or break the kettle stitches or the stitches over the bands. The backs are pasted again and then scratched diagonally from left to right, and then from right to left, being pasted after each scratching, and the paste is well rubbed into the grooves made by the scratches. It is then rubbed off, and the backs are smoothed with an old cutting board, and wiped clean with a wisp of paper shavings. A light coat of glue is given to each back, and the batch of books is left in the press for some time, preferably all night. This operation gives strength and firmness to the backs of the books.

Lining up gives stability and smoothness to the back of a book, and it consists of gluing several thicknesses of paper on to it. For the first few thicknesses, good, smooth brown paper will do, but stout cartridge paper is best for the last layer, as it offers a smoother surface to which to paste the leather. The back of the book and the hold-on back of the cover are both lined, as may be seen on examining a leather-bound volume. Flexible work is not lined, the leather being glued directly to the book.

Headbands are purchased by the foot or yard at any bookbinders' material warehouse, at prices varying according to the depth and quality of the band. These headbands are specially woven, and are cut up in pieces the width of the thickness of

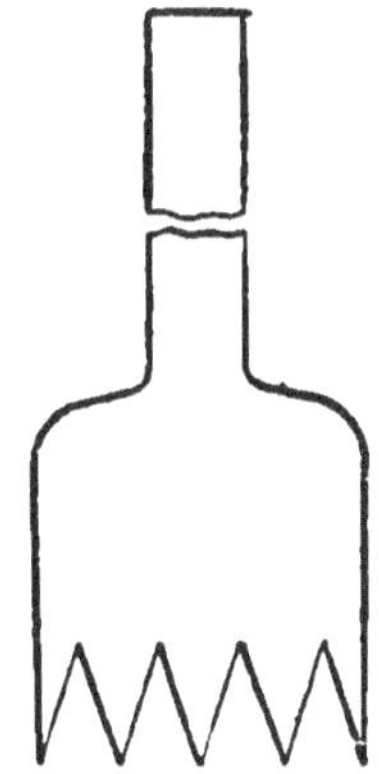

Fig. 37.—Scratching-up tool.

the book, allowing for the curve of the back, and are glued on top and bottom, the woven pattern coming level or flush with the edges. A reference to any well-bound book will at once explain the operation. Headbands are sometimes worked by hand, silk and gold and silver thread being used. The foundation may be of any substantial material. The best way to learn to make a headband will be to take an old one to pieces.

In all whole binding, and in good half morocco or half calf, it is usual to affix raised artificial bands to the back of the book. In the early days of bookbinding, saw kerfs were not made on the back of books, and the cords on which the sheets were sewn formed prominent ridges across the back after the book was covered with leather. The actual bands are never left protruding now, except in the so-called elastic work, but as raised bands take off the monotony of a plain flat back and afford scope to the finisher, artificial bands are affixed to the backs of well-bound books, the number of bands depending on the size of the book. For octavos, five is a usual number. The bottom band is farther from the tail than the top one is from the head, and this allows for the extra fillet in finishing, which is worked twice at the tail and only once at the head. Bands are usually made of narrow strips of solid stout leather carefully cut, all of one width and thickness. The space between the bands should be set off on the back with compasses, and the bands securely glued on. When this has been done the book is ready for covering.

CHAPTER V.

CUTTING BOOK EDGES.

CUTTING the edges is performed with the plough at the lying press. The operation is termed cutting in boards. The plough knife should be carefully ground and whetted, or good work cannot be done. The head or top of the book is cut first, the back being towards the operator. A cutting board is placed behind the book, and a straight runner along the millboard and level with its edge ; the book is then placed level in the press, which is screwed up tightly. When the head has been cut, the tail or bottom of the book is treated in a similar manner.

These operations are simple enough, but cutting the fore edge or front of the book presents more difficulty, as it is necessary that the curved back should first be rendered flat. This is an operation that requires considerable care, and if the amateur cannot obtain a little personal instruction on this point he is likely to spoil many books. The operator holds the book in his left hand, permitting the boards to fall back flat, and passes a piece of string once or several times round the book. He then pushes a couple of pieces of thin bevelled iron termed trindles (see Fig. 38, p. 57) between the book and the boards at the head and at the tail. Taking the book between the palms of his hands, the operator now beats the back of the book quite flat on the cheek of the press, the cord and trindles helping to keep the back flat. Having made the book flat, and having marked the front edge of the book back and front, the operator places a cutting board level with the mark at the back of the book, and another cutting board, or a long, straight runner, a little below the line on the front (or right hand), and, striking out the trindles, lowers the book into the cutting press, the millboards hanging down. The distance below the mark at which the runner is placed must be equivalent to the desired square for the board at the fore edge. When the volume is in the press, if it has been kept level, the runner must be level with the right-hand cheek, and the other cutting board must stand up for the distance of the size of the square above the left-hand cheek. When the book is correctly fixed, the press is screwed up tightly, and the front edge of the book is cut with the plough as before. When the book is taken out of the press the back will resume its convex shape, and the fore edge should present a regular concavity.

As the cutting of the edges of the book is a very important operation, the following points must be remembered. The edges must be square with the printed lines on the page, and should not be trimmed more than is necessary. The margins of white paper on a page must bear a certain proportion to each other. The printer, when preparing the pages for printing, settled the margins for the page, and fixed also the proportions. The binder cannot improve on this arrangement, but he can spoil it altogether by bad cutting. The white paper at the top of a page, measured from the type (excluding the headline) to the edge of the paper, and the white paper at the front of a page, measured from the type to the edge of the paper, should be of equal width; the white paper at the bottom of the page, measured from the type to the edge of the paper, should be about one-fourth more than the front or the top margin. Thus, if the front margin and the top margin are each 1 in., the bottom margin should be 1¼ in. ; the back margin in such a case would be $\frac{3}{4}$ in., and as this margin cannot be trimmed, the width of it compared with the other margins shows at once whether the book has been properly cut. It will be readily understood now that good and accurate folding is of the greatest importance, because the cutting of the edges of a book magnifies any errors committed in folding. The trained eye, however, is a better guide for margins than the measuring tape. The book covers

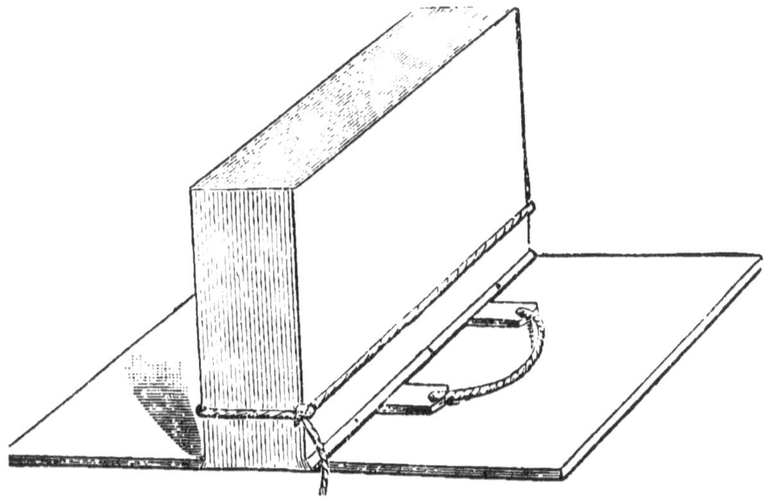

Fig. 38.—Book tied up for Cutting.

must be absolutely square to the paper, as the paper is to the print; the covers must not overhang the book too much, and the amount of overhang must be in the same proportion (the difference, of course, is only enough to be just perceptible) as the margin is to the printed page.

Books bound in cloth or in other cheap styles have their edges cut on the guillotine, as the use of the plough is too expensive for cheap repetition work.

CHAPTER VI.

COVERING BOOKS.

Books may be covered either with leather or with cloth; leather may be used either to cover the entire book, which is termed whole binding, or a strip of leather may be applied to the back only, and small pieces of leather affixed to the corners, which is termed half binding. For whole binding the leather should be cut of sufficient size to cover the book and to allow about an inch all round to turn over. For half binding a strip of leather of the desired width and rather longer than the book should be cut for the back, and four small pieces for the corners. The edges of the leather then must be very carefully pared or skived, so that no unsightly ridges can be seen. When the leather is pasted on the covers of the book the paring is done by laying the leather (flesh side uppermost) flat on a marble slab or smooth piece of board, and taking off a slanting shaving with the paring knife, which should be very sharp.

Suppose that an octavo volume is to be bound in whole morocco. The leather cover, properly pared round the edges, and rather farther in at those places that will come at the head and tail of the back, is carefully and completely coated all over on the flesh side with thick paste, and placed on the work bench with the pasted side upward, and one of the narrow edges towards the operator. The book to be covered is taken up and the boards are adjusted so that the squares are correct at the head and tail. Those portions of the string bands that have not been laced into the boards are lightly

touched with thick paste ; some binders also make
a practice of brushing over the back with thin glue.
The book is laid down on its side in the proper
place on the pasted cover, with the back from the
operator. The lower flap of the leather is drawn
over the upper millboard and turned in at the fore
edge ; and when this is done the book is turned over
and the other side of the leather also turned in at
the fore edge. The book is then rested on its fore
edge and the leather worked tight at the back with
the fingers of both hands, as shown at Fig. 39. In
this operation the leather is not only drawn close
and tight to the back crosswise by pushing it down-

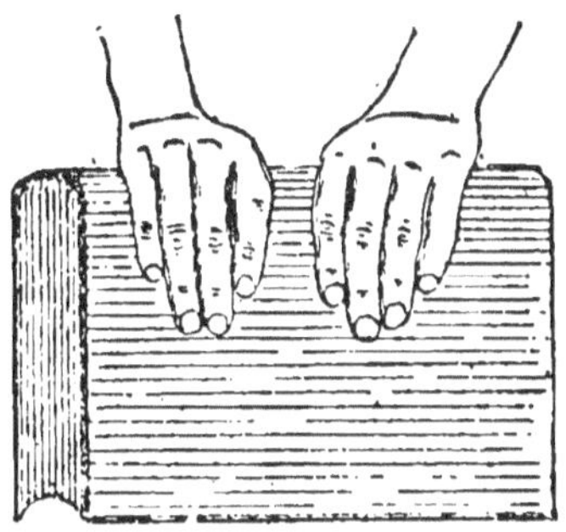

Fig. 39.—Tightening Leather on Back of Book.

ward on the millboards at each side of the book,
but it is also drawn tight longitudinally towards the
head and tail. The book next is laid on its side.
Each band should be raised alternately, and the
leather drawn tightly over its surface and rubbed
down with the palm of the hand or the folder till
quite level. The leather has now to be turned in
at the head and the tail. For this purpose the book
is stood on one end and the flap of leather A (Fig.
40, p. 60) turned over the end of the bands and also
over the loose fold of the paper which lines the back.
The other end of the book is treated similarly. It
now remains to turn in the corners. For this purpose the leather is cut off diagonally to within

rather less than ⅛ in. of the corner. This is bent
back from the book, a cutting-board placed under it,
and the diagonal edges are carefully pared and
afterwards pasted. The leather is accurately
doubled in level with the board at the head or tail,
as the case may be, and the part A (Fig. 41) pressed
tight to the other surface of the leather as shown.
Both the folder and the thumbnail can aid in bringing the leather close and level. The flap of leather
B is turned over and rubbed so that it adheres to
the board. The leather above the headband at

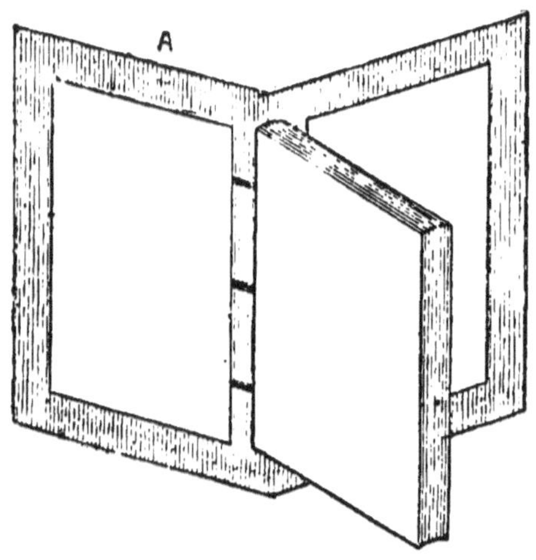

Fig. 40.—Turning in Leather at Head and Tail of Book.

both the head and tail of the book is now pulled up
a little if necessary, rubbed quite smooth with
the points of a folder, then turned down over the
headband and rubbed with the folder until it main-
tains its place. This double fold of leather above
the headband is termed the cap of the headband,
and Fig. 42 shows a section through both headband
and cap. During the operation of covering, so that
thorough contact may be ensured, the leather on the
back should be well pressed and rubbed down with
the hand and the folding-stick. The edge of the

folder also should be rubbed carefully on each side
of the bands to force the leather in at these angles
and make them clean and sharp. The book is then
tied up and left, generally for a night, till the

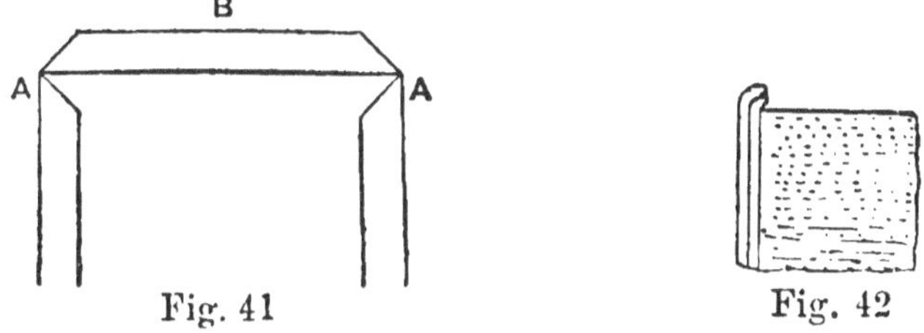

Fig. 41.—Turning in Corners of Leather.   Fig. 42.—Section
through Headband and Cap.

paste has set. Tying up is effected by first tightly
tying a loop of packthread lengthways round the
book at the joints ; that is, at that part of the book

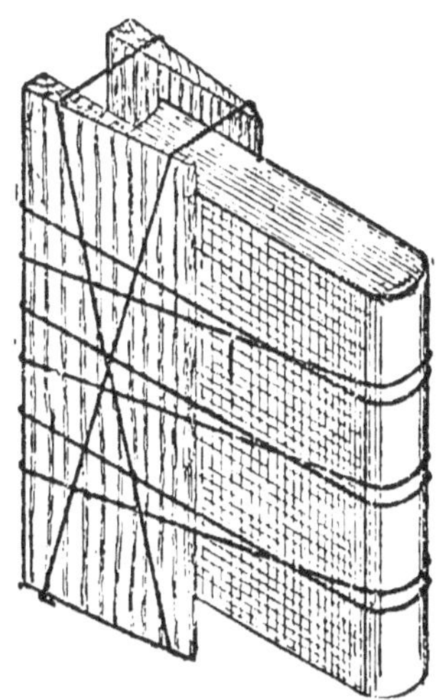

Fig. 43.—Book tied up in Boards.

where the boards are hinged to the back. A
stronger piece of twine then is wound several times
round the book, so that it passes on each side of
each band, as shown at Fig. 43. A pair of backing
or cutting boards should be tied at the fore end of

the book as shown, to prevent the string marking
the leather.

Covering with calf, goat-skin, roan, or any other
leather, is conducted in the same manner. The calf
cover must be soaked in water, carefully wrung out,
and all the creases made by the wringing smoothed
out before the skin is pasted. If the book is to be
covered with white vellum or forril, the millboards
and back should be covered with clean white paper,
or the colour of the vellum will be degraded by the
colour of the boards underneath. Half-bound books

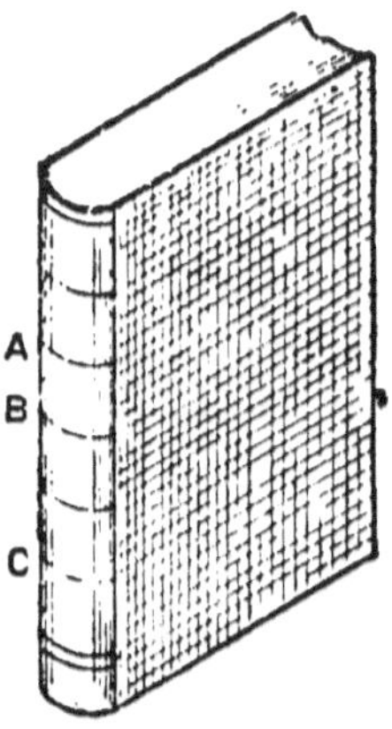

Fig. 44.—Book with Square Lettering Pieces.

are covered in the same general manner. The four
corners are first pasted and affixed, and then the back.

Books bound in morocco or roan are usually
lettered directly on the leather. But as this plan
does not answer well with calf, it is usual, when
binding in calf, to affix a small square of smooth
morocco on the back at the place where the title is
to appear, and these tablets are called lettering
pieces. They are generally scarlet, green, or purple,
and should be in contrast to the colour of the calf ;
thus, a scarlet lettering piece looks well on a book
bound in dark-brown calf, a green piece on a dark
purple, and a purple or marone piece on a fawn or

salmon colour. If there is but one lettering piece, it is usually fixed in the space between the first and second band from the head, as at A in Fig. 44. If a second piece is required to bear the number of the volume, it can be placed either at B or at C. Sometimes, when there are no raised bands, a square lettering piece is placed towards the head of the book, and below it a small round or oval piece of a different colour, as shown in Fig. 45. This is an old-fashioned method which at one time was very

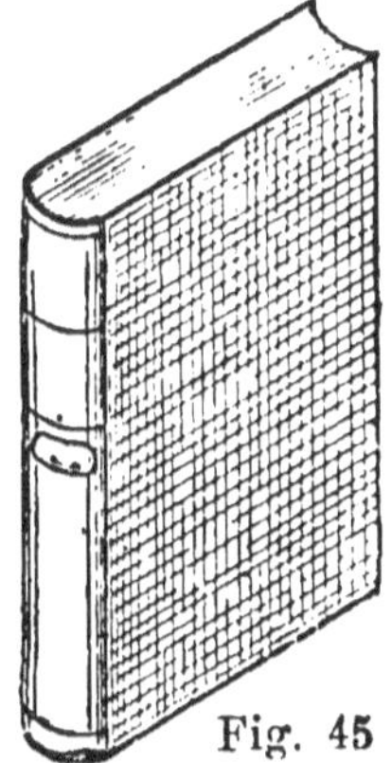
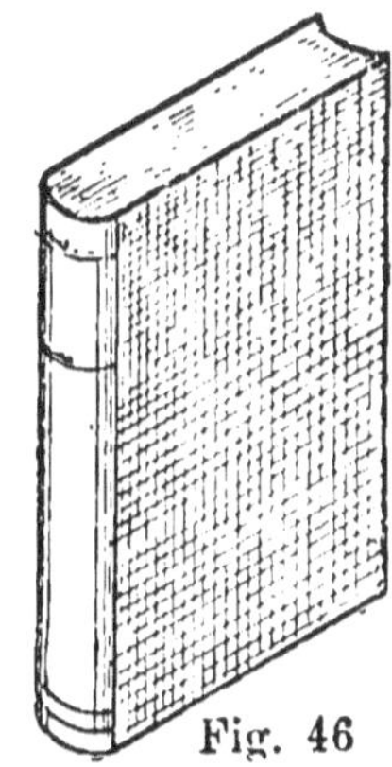

Fig. 45   Fig. 46

Fig. 45.—Book with Oval Lettering Piece. Fig. 46.—Book with Lettering Piece at the Head.

popular. For crown octavos a lettering piece towards the head is frequently adopted, as shown in Fig. 46, and, instead of filleting, the lower part of the back is tooled ornamentally. The backs of the books should be marked off for filleting before the lettering pieces are affixed. This is done by setting off the places of the fillet with a pair of compasses, and then creasing or making a slight channel at those places with the sharp edge of a thin folding-stick, taking care that the marks shall be perfectly straight and square across the back, as the finisher will be guided by them in applying his fillet roll, or pallet across the back.

Putting on sides and pasting down end papers are two processes properly belonging to forwarding, though the practice of different binders varies. Some perform these operations before the books are sent to the finishing shop; others have the finishing executed before they affix the sides and paste down the end papers; and some defer burnishing the edges until after the finishing of the book. These variations in practice are matters of convenience.

The sides of the half-bound volume may be either of marbled paper or of cloth. If the book has marbled end papers and edges, the sides should, of course, match them. Cloth sides are more durable than paper, and are much used for books that are likely to undergo hard service. Whether the cloth sides should match the leather back or contrast with it is a matter of taste. In cutting the cloth or paper the sides are cut perfectly straight along the back, and obliquely off for the corners, as at Fig. 47, the latter portions being so cut as to leave the leather corners showing beyond the sides all of exactly the same size. It is advisable to do all the cutting with a sharp-pointed knife and pair of cutting boards instead of scissors. Cloth sides are affixed with thin glue, and marbled paper sides with thin paste. The sides should be carefully rubbed down to exclude air bubbles, and turned over, and the edges made flat and square by rubbing with the folding-stick. Before pasting down the end papers, the least possible shaving should be cut off at the head, tail, and fore edge of the leaf; otherwise, as the leaf will certainly stretch a little when it is pasted and rubbed down, the pasted-down end paper might show slightly on the square of the board, which would be an imperfection in good binding. The end papers are then covered with thin paste, and are carefully rubbed down to get rid of any blisters or air bubbles. The end of the

folder may be used to press home the paper at the
joints ; if the end paper does not stick to the edge
of the board line, a hollow space, known technically
as a " pencil case," will be left, and this is considered very objectionable. The books, with the
boards or covers open, should be set up on their

Fig. 47.—Side of Cover of Half-bound Book.

heads or tails on a bench until dry, when they should
be placed between pressing boards in the standing
press and considerable pressure applied. The books
then are ready for the finisher. Gilt-edge books
must be protected by covering their edges with
paper.

CHAPTER VII.

CLOTH-BOUND BOOKS, PAMPHLETS, ETC.

WHAT in professional bookbinding is termed cloth boarding is, as has already been stated, different altogether from leather binding, but in cases where cloth is merely substituted for leather, the earlier steps of forwarding are the same as for half-bound books. The edges may be left white, or sprinkled, or gilt; it is merely a question of cost. The cloth cover is carefully cut out to size, glued over, the book laid on it, and the cloth drawn on, just as with leather coverings, pains being taken to secure adhesion everywhere and not to leave blisters. The corners are cut off and turned in as described for the morocco cover. The principal thing to be attended to in cloth work is the state of the glue and the manner of its application. The glue should be very thin and very well frothed, so that it may be applied to the cloth in such a state as to be readily and equally distributed over the surface, with no lumps and no thick or thin streaks. Cloth work is not head-banded, but a fold of the cover at the head and tail is turned in over the fold of the paper lining the back. Sometimes leather lettering pieces are placed on the back of cloth books, but this is rarely done, and generally all lettering, filleting, and other gilding is performed directly on the cloth.

Cloth boarding is the binding adopted for cheap new books, and those who practice it are known as publishers' binders. Many of the processes are nearly identical with those used in leather binding, but the work generally is fragile, and has little durability, being executed very quickly and cheaply.

Much of the work is done by machines, the folding being performed at the rate of from 1,000 to 3,000 sheets per hour, according to the character of the work. Gathering is also done with great rapidity by a machine like a revolving table, at which gatherers sit, and as the table revolves each gatherer takes a sheet from the pile as it passes. In gathering by hand, the piles of folded sheets in the order of signatures are laid out on a long table, and the gatherer passes along the table, taking a sheet from each pile until a book is made up. After collating (that is, examining each completed book to see that the sheets have been placed in their proper order), the books are slightly rolled to compress the folds. Cloth books are sewn in several different ways. If sewn on cord, the kerfs are cut with rapidly revolving circular saws, which make all the kerfs simultaneously. But it is more usual now to sew this kind of work on tapes which do not require any saw kerfs. The sewing is performed by women at the sewing press as before described. Books are also sewn by a specially contrived sewing machine in which a wire thread is employed. Such sewing can be used for ephemeral publications, for which, and for pamphlets and periodicals, it is admirably adapted, but it is not recommended for leather work.

The edges of the books next are cut with the guillotine machine. The backs then receive a coat of glue, and when this is sufficiently dry, the books are rounded and backed, and then lined on the backs with a double thickness of paper.

In preparing the cloth covers or cases the millboards, the cloth, and the stiffeners are cut to the proper size, large quantities being done at one time. The stiffeners are slips of stoutish paper of the length and breadth of the back of the book. The cloth is glued all over, the millboard laid on it, and the stiffeners are placed between them in proper position, so as to leave a slight space between its edges and those of the millboard, so that the case will fit well at the joints. The cloth is now rubbed well down on the millboards and stiffener, turned over at all the edges, and the corners are cut off and turned in also. These cases are finished at one operation at the arming press. The lettering and any ornament either for the back or sides of the case, whether gilt or blind, is attached to the platen of the press, which is heated by gas, and can be brought down forcibly by working the handle, somewhat after the manner of a hand printing-press (see Fig. 101, p. 135).

In the forwarding shop the back of the book is glued to the back of the case, and the end papers are pasted down to the boards. The books are then put in the press for a time, and when dry are ready for the bookseller's shop.

Books that are illustrated with plates independently of the text usually contain for the guidance of the binder directions for the placing of these plates, and it is of course a simple matter to follow the instructions. It must, however, first be ascertained that the margin is perfectly square and straight, and any error should be rectified by cutting with a sharp knife and straightedge. In the case of an upright picture (that is, when the inscription reads across the bottom of the page) there is diversity of practice in placing it in the book, some contending that it should occupy either the right-hand or the left-hand page, as the case may be, so as to face the descriptive text. Many publishers, however, insist that in all separately printed plates the picture when the book is open should be on the left-hand page; and this contention is, for artistic and other reasons, undoubtedly correct. In the case of longway pictures (that is, when the inscription reads along the side of the page), there is no diversity of opinion as to which is the correct position of the picture. It should always be on the left-hand page, the inscription should always read from the bottom to the top of the page, and should always be on the inner and never on the outer margin. Cases are, of course, often occurring where both printers and binders flagrantly disregard this arrangement, but the best authorities never permit a longways picture to be on a right-hand page. The plate is pasted along the edge and placed in the position it is to occupy. The visible margins on the plate should bear the same proportion to each other as the margins of the page. Double plates and maps must be folded correctly, special care being taken to see that the folds do not appear beyond the edges of the book. In some cases a guard is pasted at the fold, and in other cases the ends are pasted like single plates. The guard is preferably of stout drawing or cartridge paper, about 1 in. or 1¼ in. wide; tape or narrow linen is sometimes used. This is pasted to the section, and permits the map or double plate to open well when the book is opened.

Coloured plates, unless thoroughly dry, are very liable to stick to the protecting tissue paper generally inserted. If the plates show any disposition to stick they may be lightly dusted over with French chalk.

A binder is sometimes required to interleave a book with writing paper, the object being to give a page of white paper facing each page of print, in order, perhaps, to facilitate the making of corrections when a new edition of a book is required, or there may be other reasons. The edges (top and front) of the sheets are cut through with a knife by hand, and the writing paper having been cut and folded to the proper size, a four-page section of white paper is inserted between each four pages of printed paper. The sheets are then dealt with in the usual manner.

As regards law books, generally these are bound in a manner peculiar to themselves. The edges are left white as cut, and the books are whole or half-bound in calf of the natural colour (a kind of fawn-coloured drab). They have generally maroue-coloured or scarlet lettering pieces, and no other ornament but a plain fillet. If in half calf, the sides are usually of cloth, as such books have frequently to undergo hard wear.

Pamphlet binding may here receive attention. After pamphlets have been stitched, whether with wire or thread, the next operation is that of covering, if this is required. There are many ways of covering pamphlets, and of them the following is very economical of time—a very important item in a long job. Supposing the pamphlet to contain 16 pp. or 20 pp., proceed thus: Lay the covers out on the table with the inside uppermost and the head at the right hand, knock up a parcel of, say, twenty or fifty pamphlets, and paste or glue the backs. Paste should be used if there is time to let it dry. Set them down at the right hand, and lift one and place it down in the centre of the cover and draw the front over it. Repeat the operation throughout the job. The operator thus will be able to watch whether the covers are being drawn on straight. The front of the cover has generally more printing on it, and if there are any lines they can be kept even, and the pamphlets will have a good appearance when they are cut. If the pamphlets contain a number of pages and have been sewn, it will be best to knock them well down with the hammer before cutting them, or they will cause much trouble in the cutting. They should be well rubbed in the back with the folder, to make the covers stick properly. Pamphlets of many sections may be stitched with thread through the side, but it will be necessary to make holes for the needle to pass through. This may be done with the hammer and bradawl, or a stabbing machine may be had for the purpose. Make the first hole in the centre of the back, about midway between the printed matter and the outside margin, the other two at equal distances from the first and the head and tail of the book. However, wiring with machines has superseded this old method. After the pamphlets have been covered and properly dried, it only remains to cut their edges.

The rebinding of a book requires considerable care and circumspection, whether the book has been already bound in leather or merely cloth-boarded. The book must be very carefully taken to pieces, bands and thread being cut, and the sheets gently pulled apart, the glue being moistened if necessary. Even if the book has been badly folded in the first instance it is seldom advisable to refold the sheets unless such a measure is unavoidable. In this the binder must use his discretion. Narrow and irregular margins and crooked pages are evils, but it is quite possible to make matters worse by rashly undertaking to refold such a book. Torn leaves, often met in old books, must be carefully mended, and any missing portions of a leaf or margin should be replaced with small strips of paper carefully pasted on. Paper discoloured by age should be matched as near as possible. A perfectly clear gum should be employed for mending, or the thin transparent gummed paper that is sold for mending music may be used sometimes with advantage.

CHAPTER VIII.

ACCOUNT BOOKS, LEDGERS, ETC.

LEDGER and account bookbinding is a class of work that is hardly likely to be offered to or attempted by the amateur. Although, in a general way, the method of binding ledgers is much like that used for ordinary books, there are considerable differences in matters of detail. Strength and durability being of vital importance in a ledger, great attention is paid to the sewing, which must be very strong. Ledgers are not sewn on cords, but on strips of parchment; therefore, saw kerfs are not required. The needle is inserted at the kettle stitch, brought out on the farther side of the band, then back across the band, entered again on the near side, passed up the centre of the section to the top of the next band, and the operation already described in the case of the first band is repeated. The covers are made by pasting together thin millboard, which is then subjected to considerable pressure. Two of the boards are pasted for half their width only, and in the opening thus left are inserted the bands on which the ledger is sewn, as well as the strips of canvas or leather glued across the back. This half of the covers is then pasted, and the book with its covers is pressed till dry. Ledgers are generally furnished with spring backs. The back is usually made of thin millboard, which is warmed at the fire and worked to the shape of the back, and then glued on. For large ledgers, severals layers of millboard are glued together, each successive layer being a trifle smaller than that to which it is glued. Other differences, such as leather joints to strengthen the covers, etc., will be better understood by comparing a bound book with a ledger.

Account-book binding—or, more properly speaking, stationery binding—includes everything from the penny memorandum book to the massive ledger. Passing over the cheaper kinds of stationery, a detailed description will be given of what is considered to be the best and most workmanlike method of binding an account book. After the paper has been ruled, it is folded into sections and prepared for sewing. If the paper is what is termed hand-made, there will be two shades on every sheet: one side will appear blue, and the other white; so to prevent a blue and white appearing together when the book is opened, the paper is "faced," that is, two blue sides are made to face each other, then two white sides, and so on through the entire book. The ruler will have left four sheets unruled; these are for the end papers.

The joints of account-books may be of cloth, linen, or leather. Black glazed linen makes a good joint for general purposes. The joint is glued, and two sheets of the four already mentioned are laid upon the joint, about $\frac{1}{8}$ in. apart from each other. The other two sheets are treated in a similar manner. Four pieces of marble paper are cut to the size, glued all over, and laid on to the edge of the linen and rubbed down with the hand (nipping the papers in the press is superfluous), and hung up to dry. Meanwhile the folding of the paper has been going on, and it will be done up in three or four sheet sections, according to the make or thickness of the paper. If the sections are too thick, the leaves will start when the book is being rounded, and if they are too thin, in sewing the back will swell, owing to the quantity of thread used. The first and last section should be lined on the outside with a strip of white calico. Some binders line the inside and outside of each section with calico; this may be necessary in special cases, but for general purposes it is not to be recommended, as a book thus treated will be very stiff to open.

Account books are sewn on tapes; therefore saw kerfs are not required. For the class of work under notice a good strong twilled linen tape (known as "binding") of a grey colour, and sold in rounds, will be needed. Three or five bands, according to the size of the book, should be set up on the bench. Strips of vellum are sometimes used as bands in conjunction with the tape for heavy books. To set up strips of vellum on the bench stitch a piece of waste tape to each end of the vellum, lap the one end round the rail at the bottom of the bench and the other round the cross-bar at the top, and put a pin or a broken needle through it.

The thread must be well selected. A good linen thread 3-cord No. 18 is a very serviceable size. Wax the thread to preserve it and to make it wear better. Each section of the book must be sewn all the way up, and the needle must be brought out at the far side of the band, and introduced again at the near side, thus bringing the thread round the bands. The end papers will also have to be sewn to the book, and treated in the same manner as a section of the book. The slips, when the book is sewn, should project about $1\frac{1}{2}$ in. on each side of the back.

Gluing up the book, the work of the forwarder, is the next operation. The glue should be of good quality and thin, and tolerably hot when applied. It must be rubbed well into the sections. If the brush does not accomplish this satisfactorily, the thumb should be used for the purpose. When the glue is dry, the fore-edge should be cut, and if the edges are to be mottled instead of marbled, do the fore-edge at this point. For instructions on this part of the work see Chapter V. The book will now be ready for rounding. A greater degree of roundness should be given to it than to a letter-press book. The inside sheet of the end papers will require to be glued to the first and last leaf of the book. This should be done after rounding the back, and the book put in the standing press be-tween tins. This pressing of books with tins should always be done, especially in the case of account books, as a greater degree of solidity will thus be imparted. If the book can be left in the press over-night, so much the better.

In the morning, as soon as the glue is ready, get the book out of the press and line the back. Scraps or waste pieces of strong leather are kept for this purpose. The linings are cut to fit between the bands and the head and tail of the book. They should be long enough to extend from 2 in. to 3 in. on each side of the book. Glue the linings and the back of the book, and when attaching the lining, rub it well down with the folder to ensure it adher-ing well. The book should be screwed up in the lying press during this operation. In lining very heavy books, cover the entire back, the bands as well.

Before making the back of an account book, it will be necessary to measure for it with a strip of paper. For this purpose, lay the paper strip on the side of the book about $\frac{3}{8}$ in. from the back, bring it over the back, carry it to $\frac{3}{8}$ in. on the other side, and cut off. With this strip of paper for a guide, cut three strips of good hard millboard, a special thin but hard board for this purpose being known as " black board." The first strip must be cut exactly to the size of the paper ; the second one a trifle wider than the first ; and the third one wider still. These strips will of course be about 2 in. longer than the book. Then with strong glue fasten the strips of board together. Glue the smallest first and each larger piece in succession so that the exposed edges of each larger piece are kept clean and free from glue; press firmly and leave till dry. The back must now be rolled, a wooden roller covered with stout brown paper being necessary. The paper is glued at one end and fastened to the roller. Heat the back thoroughly over a gas flame or a bundle of lighted shavings, and allow the heat to penetrate the boards, taking care to prevent burning. When the back is hot and pliable, place it in the roller and give one sharp turn; then reverse quickly and give another turn. It may require to be reversed several times to keep all the parts in place during rolling. Now roll up tightly, and with a flat board, such as a backing board, roll the back over the bench several times, pressing heavily all the time; then set it aside to dry. The diameter of the roller should be about half the width of the back itself. When the back is thoroughly dry it should be well rubbed down on the edges and forced on the back of the book. The waste sheet of the end-paper of one side of the book is now glued and folded back up to the linings and brought over the back. The other side is also glued and brought over the back in the same manner, and all are well rubbed down, a board being placed on each side of the book close to the back and the whole put into a press and given a good nip. This will make all flat and draw the back tight. The linings and end-papers form a kind of hinge on each side, and with these the side boards are fastened. Make a cut in this hinge on both sides at the top and bottom (thus there are four cuts), about 2 in. in from the outside. This is to allow for turning in the cover. The boards for account book backs are made of several thicknesses, and the inside board of the series is generally a thin one; in making, this is only glued half-way. Now, after squaring up the boards, they are added to the book by gluing this part on both sides and inserting the hinge in the split, allowing the two small pieces to remain outside. When both boards are put on, the book is again pressed; when dry it is taken out, and is then ready for covering in the usual manner.

To allow time for the glue to set, cut the ends of the book, and mottle them as directed for the fore-edge (see Chapter IX.).

It will be necessary to take great care in cutting the ends of an account book, as owing to the deep groove in the fore-edge, caused by the rounding of the back, the paper is apt to break at the corner. This can be avoided by padding up the fore-edge with waste paper.

There is nothing special about the manner of covering account books. They are covered in much the same manner as letterpress books, with the exception of knatching, which is done as soon as the cover is turned in. A pair of knatching boards, that is, boards with a projecting piece about the thickness of a small cane screwed along the top edge—is placed in the grooves made between the back and the boards on the sides of the book, and the whole screwed up in the lying press. After knatching, a cord is tied round from end to end and the heads are set. The setting of the heads should be carefully attended to, as, when properly done, the book is much enhanced. There should not be any hammer or folder marks on the edge of the book. When the cover has become dry, the cloth sides are put on if the book is half-bound, and the end papers are glued up; a strip of thin board is placed close up to the joint on both sides of the book during this process: this acts as a lever, and causes the book to spring when being opened. After gluing up, the book is put in the standing press, and left there all night if possible, and the forwarder's work is practically done.

Account books, like letterpress books, are covered in various styles. They are half-bound in sheep, goat, calf, morocco, Persian, and full bound in the same materials. When covered in goat or calf, it is generally the flesh side of the skin that is on the outside. Full calf with green vellum corners rounded, instead of being cut square, is a good style. Full calf, with Russia bands laced with white vellum, is very commendable for large books, but does not add so much to the strength, it is believed, as is commonly supposed ; do not leave the lacing inside the board, as when glued up it presents a very bad appearance. Instead of this, open the board and lay it down on an iron block, and beat it well with the hammer on the inside so as to close the holes well up, and after drawing the lacing as tight as possible, cut off the laces and beat again and again, until not a trace of roughness is seen upon the board.

In finishing account books, the ordinary leathers are treated as described in Chapter XIII. Rough calf and goat are cleaned by rubbing with bath-brick. The black lines are put on with iron liquor carried in a sponge tied to the end of a piece of whalebone or stick, and held upon the roll as it is being run upon the backs or sides of the book. These hints on finishing will be quite intelligible after reading Chapter XIII.

CHAPTER IX.

COLOURING, SPRINKLING, AND MARBLING BOOK EDGES.

THE edges of a book may be ornamented in a variety of ways, and this ornamentation is necessary almost, because plain edges rapidly become dirty. The forms of decoration now commonly employed are colouring, sprinkling, marbling, and gilding. The style of decoration is governed by the character of the binding, and the character of the binding has generally some reference to the character of the book.

Colouring the edges of a book in a self or sole colour is not very much in vogue at the present day, except for prayer-books, hymnals, and devotional books, the edges of which are sometimes coloured red. But many years ago the practice was a very fashionable one, some of the commonest colours, after red, being dull green, yellow, and blue. The colour, which should be well ground, is mixed with a little glaire and oil, and if one coat is not enough, the first coat must be thoroughly dry before the second coat is applied. The book must be knocked up even at the head and laid on the edge of the press or table, the left hand holding it tightly to prevent the colour running in. The colour may be applied with a small sponge passed evenly towards the back one way, and the fore-edge the other, to prevent the colour forming in a mass at the back or fore-edge. The tail of the book is treated in the same manner as the head. For the fore-edge the boards will have to be thrown back and a cutting board held firmly above. The colour is more liable to run in at the fore-edge, therefore a little more care will be necessary. If a number of volumes are to have the same edge, they can be done by simply placing them one above the other. Sometimes binders put their books in the lying press when colouring them as a precaution against the colour running in. In applying colour with a sponge or brush, there is this risk of the ink finding its way between the leaves, and it may be found safer to use a spray producer such as is shown by Fig. 48. In this figure A is a 1-oz. bottle, B and C are

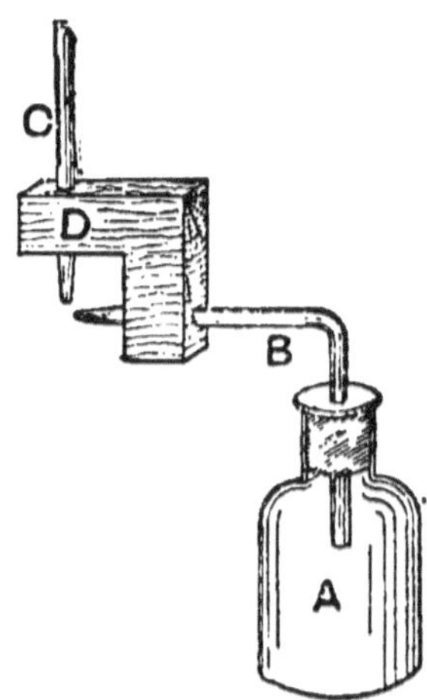

Fig. 48.—Sprayer for Colouring Book Edges.

two pieces of glass tube about ⅛-in. bore, and D is a small piece of wood or metal. When A is filled with ink or dye, upon blowing down C a fine shower of spray is directed downwards. A far neater arrangement made wholly of metal can be bought very cheaply. Having obtained a suitable sprayer, cover the book to be coloured with paper, leaving only the edges bare; take the spray producer, hold it over the book, blow down C, Fig. 48, and the book will soon be coloured with an even coat. If this is done for a short time only it will give a speckled appearance

If a few grains of rice or such-like be spread along the edges before the colour is applied, the effect will be similar to marbling ; and if it is done first with one colour—say red— the grains of rice shaken off, some more dropped on, and then done with some other colour—say blue—the result will be very pleasing indeed. Another method is to dip a tooth-brush in dye, hold it over the edges of the book. and then draw a knitting-needle from one end of the bristles to the other.

Sprinkled edges usually are adopted for half-calf and cloth work. Ordinary red sprinkle may be made of any cheap dark red pigment carefully ground. Armenian bole (a red earth brought from the East) is usually employed, but red ochre or Indian red will do. The Armenian bole is poured in a small heap on the centre of the grinding slab, a depression is made in the centre of the heap, and a lump of thin paste and a few drops of sweet oil are placed therein. The whole is then mixed well together with a palette knife into a rather moist, red paste. The bulk of the mixture is then pushed on one side, a lump about the size of a walnut being placed in the centre of the slab and ground with the muller, working with a circular motion, until all grittiness has vanished and the paste is quite impalpable. When sufficient of the paste has been ground, it is placed in the sprinkle pot, which is a red earthenware jar large enough to contain as much sprinkle as is likely to be needed. Water is then added, and the sprinkle well stirred until the paste is all dissolved. The books to be sprinkled are ranged side by side on a bench and a cord put round them, or, better, they are screwed up in the lying press. The operator then takes up a brushful of sprinkle, squeezes out the surplus on the edge of the pot, and strikes the brush (keeping it over the pot) across a short thick stick, held in the left hand, until the brush is only slightly charged and the spots or drops thrown off are very small and fine. He then in the same way, keeping his hands tolerably high, strikes the brush forcibly against the stick, so as to send down a shower of very small red spots upon the edges of the book beneath. Considerable practice is required for the proper performance of apparently so simple an operation as sprinkling.

Although the method of preparing red sprinkle has been described at length, the amateur will find that almost any dye or stain (such as Judson's dyes), diluted if necessary, can be used. Some binders use ordinary writing ink even. A method of ornamenting book edges that permits of a great variety of treatment is to scatter over the edges, before

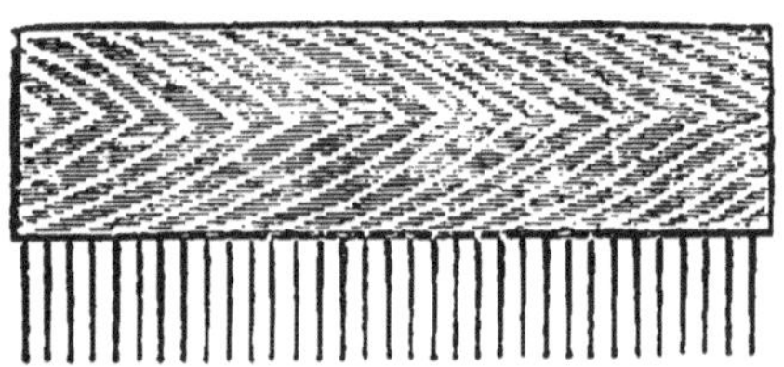

Fig. 49.—Marbling Comb.

sprinkling, rice grains and small seeds, or small paper patterns of various shapes. By altering the arrangement of the seeds or patterns and sprinkling with a different colour a variety of effects can be produced. This method is noted on p. 81. The edges of a book should be burnished after sprinkling, colouring, or marbling.

Another method of sprinkling, but one that is not recommended, is this : A small brush like a sixpenny gum brush, dipped in colour, is held tightly beween the finger and thumb of the left hand near to the end of the hair. The forefinger of the right hand strikes the projecting hair with a movement similar to that employed when playing a Jew's harp. The brush does not hold much colour owing to the manner in which it is held in the fingers, and the workman in consequence loses time.

One, two, three, or any number of colours may be used to the same edge, and many combinations have a pleasing effect. A great deal depends upon the taste of the workman.

A good substitute for marbling, and one which looks much better than sprinkling, is mottling. This is done with an open-holed sponge filled with colour and daubed lightly over the edge, leaving the natural marks of the sponge. The edge may be coloured all over first, or it may be mottled on the white edge alone. Red and black makes a good combination. This style of edge is not very suitable

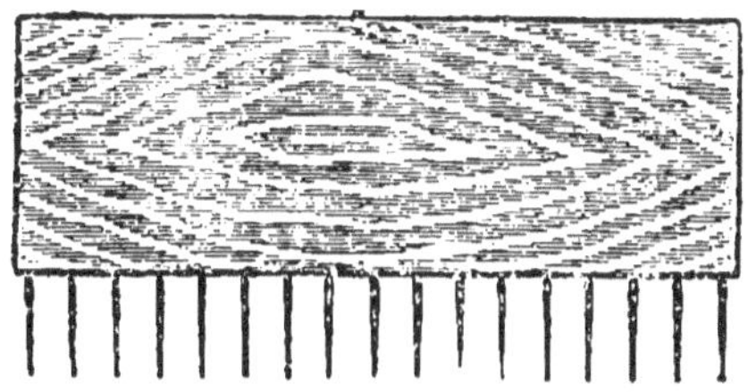

Fig. 50.—Marbling Comb.

for letterpress work, but it looks its best on heavy account books. It is certainly much more beautiful than some of the Dutch marble patterns seen upon this class of work.

The marbling of book edges and the making of marbled papers is, as may be judged from the finished results, a difficult art. Some bookbinders are able to do their own marbling, but, as a rule, except, perhaps, in country places, marbling is generally entrusted to professional marblers, who do the work very cheaply and expeditiously. Amateurs will do well if they also employ the professional marbler, for though the work is not beyond the capacity of a painstaking and artistic amateur, it will for the majority be found tedious, messy, and probably unsatisfactory. But though marbling requires some skill, yet it is at the same time a simple process, and the apparatus and

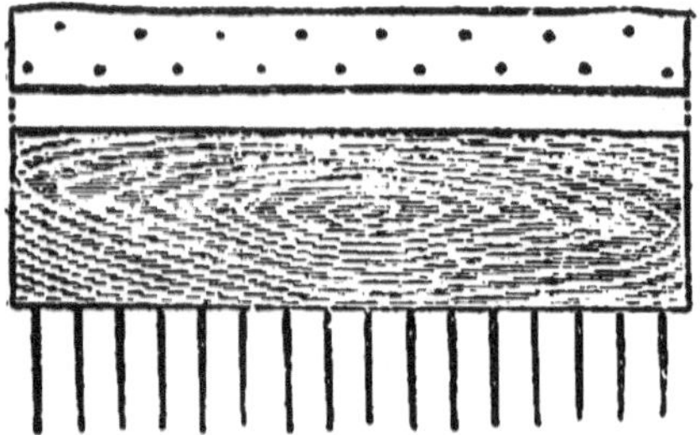

Fig. 51.—Marbling Comb.

materials may be described in a few words, all that is necessary being a shallow wooden water-tight trough, a flat piece of wood, equal in length to the breadth of the trough and about 3 in. broad, a number of combs (Figs. 49 to 51) the teeth of which are of different widths, wooden rakes, cups, jugs, bottles, brushes for the colours, a large earthenware

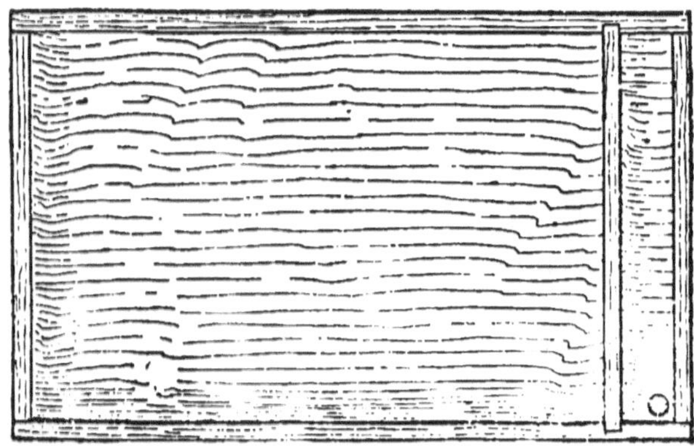

Fig. 52.—Marbling Trough.

bucket or pan, a bunch of birch rods, and a marble slab and muller for grinding the colours. Thus it is quite an easy matter for the marbler to construct his own apparatus. The trough is generally of well-seasoned oak; the size is immaterial, but must be larger than the work to be done. Useful dimensions are about 30 in. by 18 in. or 20 in. by $2\frac{1}{2}$ in. It should be made of stuff sufficiently thick to prevent warping, and about 3 in. of its length should be cut off by a sloping partition, which should be about $\frac{1}{8}$ in. below the sides. In the right-hand corner of this part a waste hole should be bored and stopped by a cork (see Fig. 52). The joints must be well made and stopped with marine glue or other water-

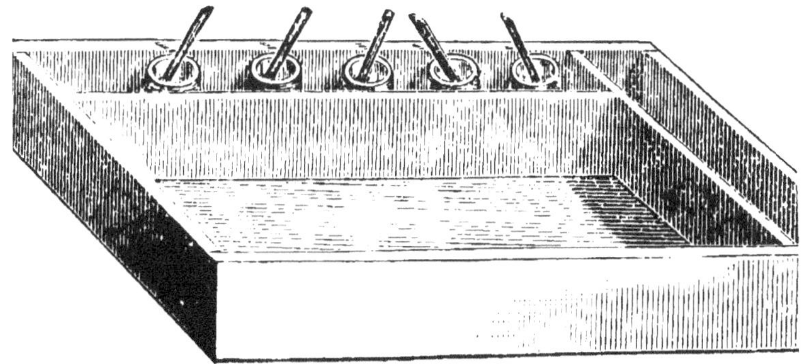

Fig. 53.—Marbling Trough and Colour Pots.

proof material. Fig. 53 shows a marbling trough partitioned off to hold colour bottles.

Gum-tragacanth or gum-dragon is the binding gum used, and it should be large, white, and flaky; dark brown lumps must be rejected. To prepare the gum, in a large earthen pan, glazed inside, and capable of containing, say, 12 gal. of water, put 1 lb. of gum-dragon, and on this pour 2 gal. of soft water (rain water if possible). Stir it every few hours with a clean birch broom (bunch of birch rods) kept for this purpose, breaking the lumps and adding water as the gum thickens. The gum requires from two to four days to dissolve properly, and must then be strained through a fine hair sieve before use. Other materials from which marbling size may be made are linseed, flea-seed, and carrageen, or Irish moss, but gum dragon cannot be excelled for everyday work.

Generally, the marbling colours are the same as those used for painting, both in oil and distemper. They should be procured in the dry state and ground by the marbler himself, although colours are to be had ground and ready for use and put up in air-tight jars. Following is a list of colours: Reds—drop lake, peach-wood lake, vermilion, rose pink, and burnt Oxford ochre. Yellows—lemon chrome, Dutch pink, and raw Oxford ochre. Brown—Turkey (burnt) umber. Blues—indigo, Chinese blue, ultramarine, and Prussian blue. Blacks—vegetable lampblack and drop ivory black. Orange—orange lead and orange chrome. White—China clay, pipe-clay, flake white, and Paris white.

Drop lake is the most beautiful and expensive of the reds, the different shades being scarlet, crimson, and purple. The scarlet possesses a brilliancy greater than that of any other colour, and is sold in the form of small cones or drops. To select a good quality, break one of the little drops and try the broken part on the tongue. If it takes up the moisture from the tongue without any inclination to adhere, it may be purchased. Vermilion is very heavy, and is seldom used except in combination with some other colour. Rose pink, a very useful colour, is chalk or whiting coloured with Brazil wood ; it is a fugitive colour, quickly fading on exposure to heat or even to the atmosphere, but with Chinese blue or indigo it makes a good purple. Burnt ochre is extensively used either by itself or in combination with other colours ; mixed with black it makes a good brown, and with blues various shades of olive can be obtained. Wood lake is a damp colour, and can be used without grinding, being made almost exclusively for marbling. It is the best red for general purposes, and has an appearance almost equal to drop lake. The most useful blue is indigo. It is not by any means a bright colour, but if of the best quality it is one of the most durable. It is invaluable for producing greens and purples. Chinese blue is a necessary colour, but it is not very durable. It must be well ground, and with the addition of varying proportions of white nearly every shade of blue can be produced. Vegetable black will not produce a black for marbling except in combination with double its weight of indigo; it is much used. Orange lead, a very heavy colour, is but little used except for the edges of account books. White is not much required, as with gall and water white spots can easily be produced; however, China clay and pipe-clay are used where necessary.

For grinding colours in the dry state a marble slab and muller must be procured. Large quantities are treated in a colour mill, which is simply a pair of porphyry rollers rotating in opposite directions close together. The colour has to be passed through several times before the proper degree of fineness is reached. After being ground, the colours are mixed in a cup with water. Besides the gum or size and colours, ox-gall, ammonia, spirits of wine, and oil will be required. Get a gall-bag from the butcher and cut a hole in the bottom to allow the gall to run into a bottle. Gall when new is often thick, but it will thin and improve with age. For the bottle get a well-fitting cork, and cut two pieces out of the sides opposite each other; then put the cork tightly in the bottle, and, without removing the cork, when the bottle is turned up a drop at a time will come out. The ammonia and spirits of wine must be kept tight with ground glass stoppers. Some of the colours require a little bees-wax to prevent them rubbing off and to aid in the burnishing afterwards. It must be added while grinding. To prepare it, chop a small piece of beeswax fine, and place it in a small tinned iron or enamelled vessel on a stove until it is melted. Then pour gradually into it some spirits of turpentine, stirring all the time until it acquires the consistency of honey. Allow it to cool, when it can be added to any colour and ground with it when necessary.

The operation of marbling may now be described. With the size a little thicker than good milk, fill the trough to within $\frac{1}{2}$ in. of the top, pouring it through the sieve. Take the skimmer (the flat piece of wood already mentioned) and draw it over the surface of the size ; if considerable resistance is felt, the size is too thick. Throw on a few spots of colour ; if these lose their shape and appear to be attracted to the sides of the trough, the size may be considered too thin. Again, if the colours crack and are a long time spreading, the size is too thick. Put into each cup or pot of colour a few drops of gall and stir it well with a small brush, which should be provided for each cup. There must also be a cup of gall and water only, with a brush.

It will be impossible here to set out in detail the manipulation of the colours to produce all the numerous patterns of marbling, but one or two of the commonest or best known designs will be described. Brown shell is a simple pattern, being a brown marble with red, yellow, and black veins. As the brown is required to spread on the size more than the other colours, it must be thicker, and it must have more gall mixed with it and a few drops of olive oil to cause the shell to be formed. Test each colour separately on the trough, skim the surface, and allow the waste to go over into the receptacle at the end of the trough. Then with the red brush sprinkle the entire surface until it is well covered ; follow with the yellow and the black, and finish with the brown, which will spread in shell-like spots lighter in the centre than at the edges, driving the other colours into veins. The shell effect will vary with the amount of gall in the brown, and the larger the shell the finer the veins. As to the quantity of oil, if there is too little the colour will part and produce holes here and there.

Next the book can be dipped, as in Fig. 54. Resting the arms on the trough, dip the book from the back to the fore-edge, making a half-circle movement with the two hands. If the book is dipped too much an unsightly mark will be left on the fore-edge. After dipping, turn the book sharply towards the body and blow strongly over the edge to get rid of the surplus size. Sometimes it may

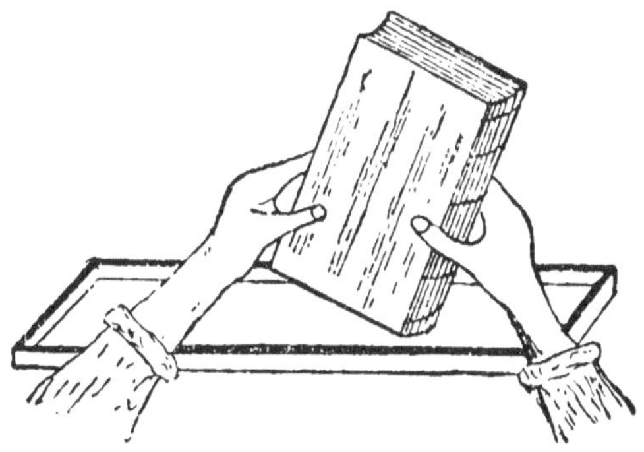

Fig. 54.—Marbling Book Edges.

be necessary to wash the size off. To do this, fill the mouth with clean water and squirt it over the edge, or pour the water from a cup. All these operations must be performed quickly ; a slow marbler will never be successful. If the trough is big enough, the three edges may be dipped one after the other ; if not, the design must be thrown on three times, the size being skimmed after each. The pattern can be varied indefinitely by changing, first the vein colours and then the body colour, making green shell, red shell, etc.

The Spanish pattern is very common, and is known by a peculiar light and shade effect of the body or top colour. To produce brown Spanish

with red, yellow, blue, and black veins, the colours
are prepared as already described ; but it may be
necessary to add more gall to some, the general rule
being to have each colour richer in gall than that
preceding it. The brown, of course, must be thick-
est, and should have more gall than the others.
First throw on the red, then the yellow, and follow
with the blue and the black ; sprinkle all freely, and
distribute them evenly over the entire surface. Now
with a brush well filled with brown start throwing
on the colour at the left-hand corner, working to
and from the body, and taking care not to go over
the same place twice. Finish throwing on at the
right corner farthest away. Dip the edge, but in
doing so give it a wave-like motion—that is, dip
about 1 in. of surface and draw backwards slightly
towards the right ; then dip another portion and
draw back ; repeat until the entire edge has been
dipped.

For nonpareil pattern a peg-rake and comb are
necessary. The peg-rake is simply a piece of wood
with pegs stuck into it. To make it, on a strip of
wood longer than the trough mark the length of
the trough, leaving equal distances at each end.
Divide the marked length equally, make a number
of holes about $1\frac{1}{2}$ in. apart, and in these insert
taper wooden pegs about 3 in. long. Leave one
peg out at the end, so that the rake can be moved
lengthwise the width of a peg space. The pegs
must reach to the bottom of the trough. The comb
is made in much the same way, but is only a little
longer than the breadth of the trough. The teeth
are of pin-wire, and may run from four to twelve
pins to the inch (see Fig. 49, p. 82). They should
just reach to the top of the colour when the wooden
part of the comb touches the upper edges of the
trough. All the colours for this pattern should have
about the same amount of gall and should be as
nearly as possible of the same thickness, as all are

intended to spread equally. First sprinkle or throw on the red so as to cover the entire surface ; then throw on the black, then the yellow, then the blue, and lastly the top colour of whatever shade may be desired. Next put the rake into the solution at the far side of the trough and draw it carefully to the near side, and, without lifting it out, shift its position the width of a peg and push it back again and lift it out. Rest the wooden part of the comb on the edges of the trough at the left-hand side, and draw it carefully along until the comb reaches the right-hand side, allowing the pins just to touch the colour ; the pattern is then complete, and the book may be dipped with a steady hand as before described.

CHAPTER X.

MARBLING BOOK PAPERS.

THE following information on marbling paper is in·tended to supplement that already given in the previous chapter.

Gum-tragacanth should alone be used as a size, for most of the troubles in marbling arise from the use of an inferior gum or the inclusion of some other ingredient with the size. Good bright colours must also be used, and must be well ground; in fact, when a colour seems intractable, sometimes the best remedy is to put it on the slab again and grind it.

When preparing the colours specially for marbling paper, a little beeswax is added, about 1 oz. to the pound of the colour being sufficient. This prevents the colour rubbing off on the hand, and causes the paper to take a better glaze when being milled or rolled. Some colours require more than others, the greens and blues perhaps requiring most wax.

The illustrations here given show well-known patterns; but before describing them it may be stated that if, instead of a common white paper, one covered with a coloured enamel or gold or silver is used some very beautiful effects can be produced.

Fig. 55 illustrates a pattern of marble paper called "Nonpareil." To produce this pattern, besides the colours and a brush for each, a peg-rake and fine comb will be required. Into each cup of colour, carefully ground and mixed with water, put a few drops of gall and stir well with the brush to be

used. Skim the surface of the trough, and throw
or sprinkle on the colour by beating the brush
against an outstretched finger of the left hand or
against an iron pin held in the left hand. Begin
with red, and sprinkle this so as to cover the entire
surface of the size in the trough, following with
black, yellow, or orange and blue, and finish with
a top colour, which may be left to the fancy of the
operator. Rake the colour with the peg-rake ; that
is, put the rake into the solution at the front of
the trough and push it back, then move it to the
right about the width of a peg and draw it to the

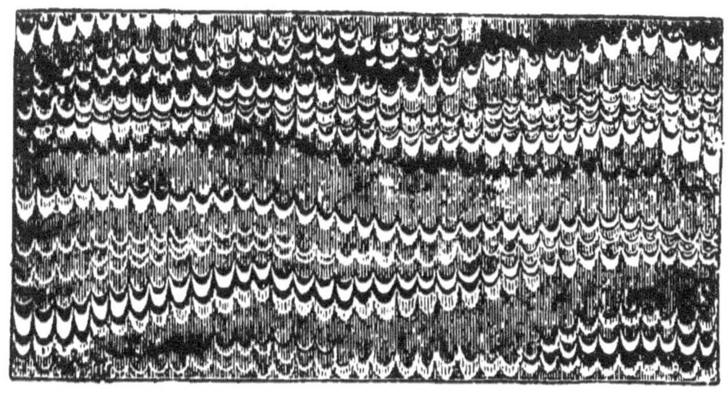

Fig. 55.—Nonpareil Marble.

front again, and lift it out. The colour will now
lie in regular streaks across the breadth of the
trough. The pegs must reach to the bottom of the
trough. Now draw the fine comb (Fig. 49, p. 82)
carefully through the colour from left to right, and
the pattern then is ready to be taken up on the
paper.

To place a sheet of paper on the marbling
colour, as the latter lies in the trough, and lift it
again after it has taken up the colour requires
some skill. By two opposite corners take up
a flat sheet of paper, hold it over the trough
until confident that the hands are in proper con-
trol, lower the right hand until it rests on the side

of the trough, and allow merely the corner of the
paper to come in contact with the solution, at the
same time lowering the left hand slowly until the
entire sheet is on the surface, and the left hand
resting against some portion of the trough. Then
raise the right hand until the sheet has been lifted
off. If the paper is too large to manage in this
way, allow it to lie on the solution, and place
across the trough from front to back a light rod
such as a lath, taking hold of the sheet by the
two right-hand corners and placing it over the rod ;
then by gently raising the rod, lift the paper off

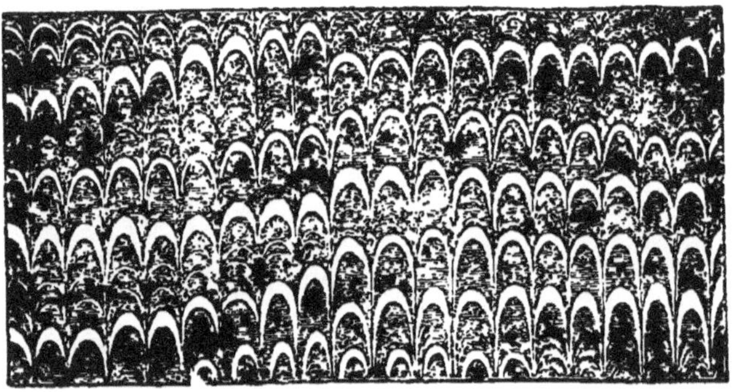

Fig. 56.—Reversed Nonpareil Marble.

the trough and spread it out flat or hang it up to
dry. If the paper is lowered too quickly, the air
will get under it and produce white spots ; and if,
when the paper lies on the trough, attempt is made
to get the air out, unsightly marks will be formed.
The varieties of this pattern are infinite ; for instance, any number of colours may be used, or only
one colour, hence there is blue nonpareil, black nonpareil, etc.

Reversed nonpareil is illustrated by Fig. 56,
and for this it is usual, although not necessary, to use
a wider comb (shown by Fig. 50, p. 83), which in
this instance will be drawn through the colour from
right to left.

Fig. 57 is a variety called "Wave Nonpareil."
For this, after the pattern has been produced as already described, another comb is drawn though the
colour from right to left with a definite zigzag
movement, so as to produce even rows, which when
viewed diagonally will appear as squares. The
comb for this pattern is shown at Fig. 51, p. 84.
It may be described as a double comb, as will be
seen from the plan, the teeth of the second row
being set to come exactly in the centre of the
spaces in the first row. The teeth should not be

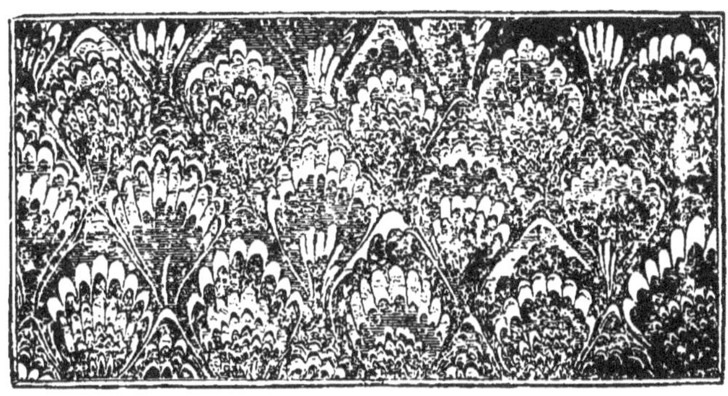

Fig. 57.—Wave Nonpareil Marble.

less than 1 in. apart, and the second row should
be at the same distance behind the first.

A very striking modification of this pattern is
called "Fancy Dutch" (Fig. 58). It may be produced with three colours only and gall and water,
the colours being red, black, and a fancy blue (say
turquoise blue). Throw on a little of the red first,
and follow with black in about the same proportion, but somewhat thicker, and with more gall,
so that it may spread and produce larger spots.
The blue must be still thicker than the black, as
it is required to spread still more. Finish with a
fairly liberal supply of gall and water, which must
spread more than any of the colours. This done,

rake as for nonpareil, and with the double comb finish the design.

If, instead of a white paper, a gold surface paper is used, the effect is really beautiful, as so much

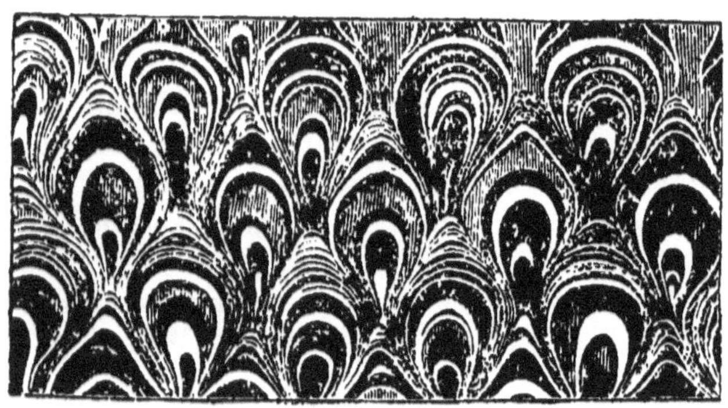

Fig. 58.—Fancy Dutch Marble.

of the gold surface is seen, owing, of course, to the gall and water having been used. It need not be stated that the size should be clean, otherwise much of the brilliancy will be lost.

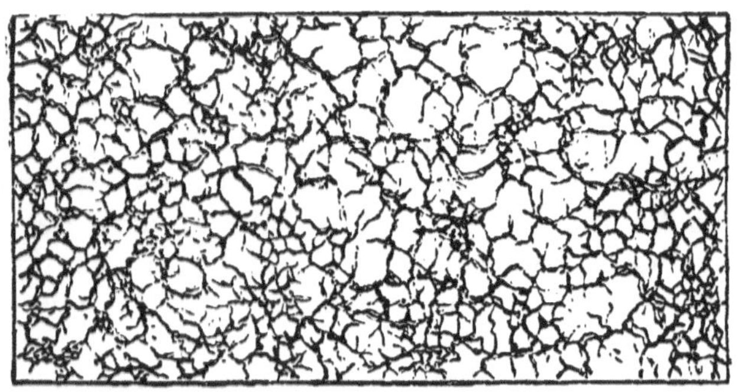

Fig. 59.—Italian Marble.

A very simple pattern, called "Italian" (Fig 59), may, if desired, be produced with one colour and gall and water. Take red, for instance, and with this cover the entire surface of the trough; now with a large brush filled with gall and water sprinkle carefully so as to produce very fine white spots.

The brush used for this is an ordinary glue or

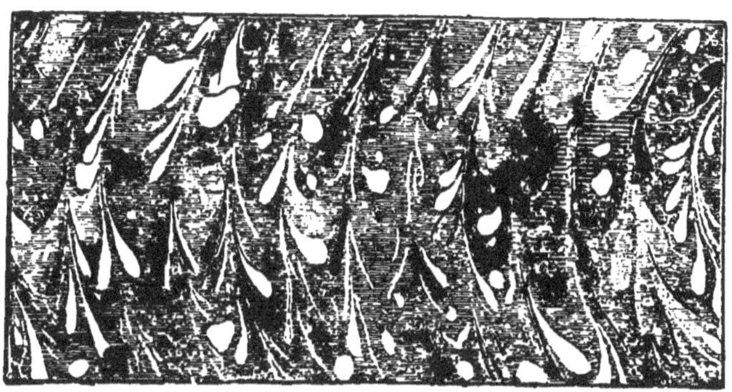

Fig. 60.—Dutch Antique Marble.

paste brush with an iron ring, and it should be beaten against an iron pin as usual. The spots may be made of irregular sizes by first having the brush fairly wet with the gall and water, and afterwards

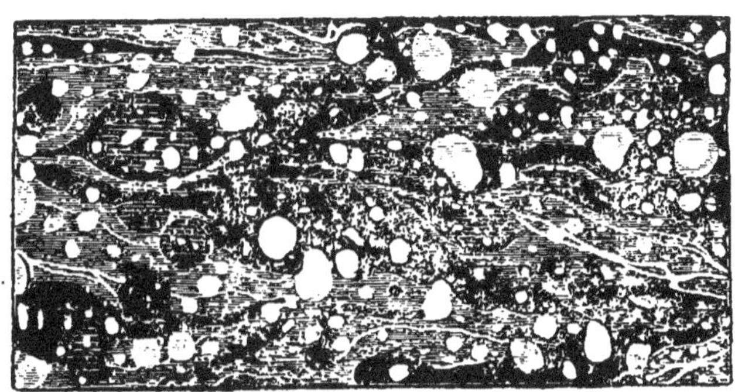

Fig. 61.—Antique Spot Marble.

almost dry, in both cases going over the whole trough while sprinkling.

Dutch antique pattern shown by Fig. 60 is another modification of the nonpareil series, and the colours should be of the best, so that they

G

may be as bright as possible. They should be of about the thickness of cream. and are put on the trough with little sticks or quills in sloping streaks. For instance, put on pairs of strokes over the whole trough, and between these double strokes put a stroke of say orange or yellow; then fill the wider spaces with green, blue, or black as desired, and draw a wide comb through to complete the pattern. If a sprinkle of gall and water is given before drawing through the comb, and a gold or silver

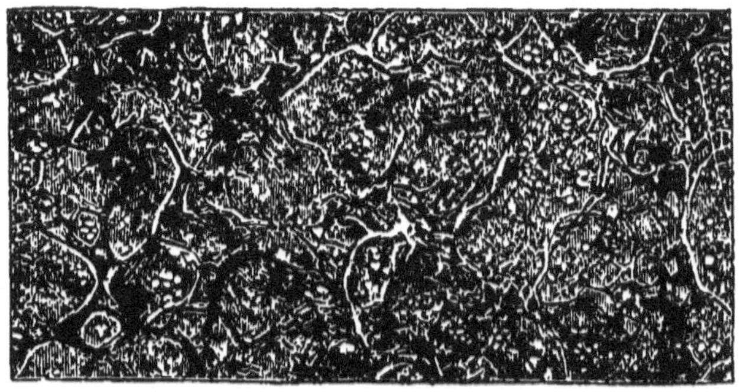

Fig. 62.—West End Marble.

paper is used, the effect will be found to be much enhanced.

Antique spot pattern (Fig. 61) is capable of much variation; the spot, for instance, may be white, pink, green, or gold. To produce it, the colours red, black, and yellow may be thrown on in the same or varying quantities and raked once up and down; afterwards another colour, blue or green, may be thrown on; then the pink for the spot, or gall and water, which will produce white if white paper is used, or gold if a gold surface paper is preferred.

West End pattern, shown by Fig. 62, is also capable of much variation, but commonly consists of two prominent colours besides the veins, one of the colours, generally the darker, being spotted finely with white. To produce this pattern, mix the colours red, black, and yellow, or as desired, for veins, and throw them on the trough, red first. Then mix, say brown, with a larger proportion of gall and sprinkle it on in large, full spots, so as to drive the other colours into veins. Now with a large brush, well filled, sprinkle gall and water over the entire surface. When well beaten out against the iron pin, the brush will produce very fine spots. Then take some white and mix it with

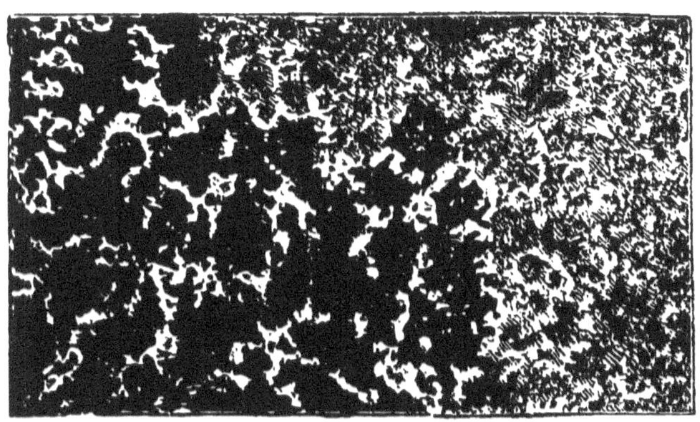

Fig. 63.—Machine-pattern Marble.

the brown so as to make it lighter, adding also a drop or two of gall; sprinkle this on full so as to produce large light spots, which complete the pattern.

Some of the newer patterns of marble papers are produced by mechanical means. One machine works somewhat like the air-brush, the colour being blown on to the paper and making a pattern like Fig. 63.

It is often necessary to size the paper after marbling, and before milling or glazing, and the best way to do this is to fill the trough with size and place the paper on it as for marbling. Of the many sizes, glue is always the basis. An old-fashioned recipe may be quoted : " Take of the best white soap 2 lb., put it into a large copper with about 20 gals. of water, and when it is quite dissolved add thereto about 4 lb. of best glue, keeping the whole constantly stirred to prevent burning. When both are quite dissolved strain into a tub, and when cool the mixture is ready for use." After sizing, the paper is passed through a calendar, that is a machine with polished steel rollers and with appliances for heating, so as to give a good gloss to the paper.

CHAPTER XI.

GILDING BOOK EDGES.

GILDING is the most beautiful method of ornamenting the edges of books; it suits almost any colour and any binding, and may be carried out in a variety of ways so as to produce many beautiful effects. Gilding is not mere ornamentation; it is also the best preservative that can be applied to book edges. Dust cannot penetrate between the leaves of gilt-edged books, decay is retarded if not altogether prevented, and the action of fire is resisted to a remarkable extent; it is for this last reason that the edges of ledgers are sometimes very thickly gilt. Among the many varieties of gilding may be mentioned gilt on colour, in which the edges are fanned out and coloured, and then gilt. Red is the colour most generally preferred, hence the common expression " gilt on red," or " red under gold "; but other colours are used. Gilding is also done on marble; it is called marbling under gilt, and as may be imagined, when well done is very beautiful. Book edges are also gilt and tooled, tools of a fine pattern being chosen and used warm.

The tools used by the edge gilder for ordinary plain gilding are the gilding press, which has long screws, a steel scraper, a gold cushion, gold knife, tip, burnisher, and a flat brush. The materials required are gum, Armenian bole, diluted glaire, and gold leaf.

In shops where gilding is done only occasionally, the ordinary lying press may be used in place of the gilding press. But where large quantities of work are executed it is usual to have a special press of the kind shown by Fig. 64.

The ordinary steel scraper is shown by Fig. 65, and is simply a flat piece of steel about $\frac{1}{32}$ in. thick. The scraper can easily be made from a broken knife, which should be ground up in the same way

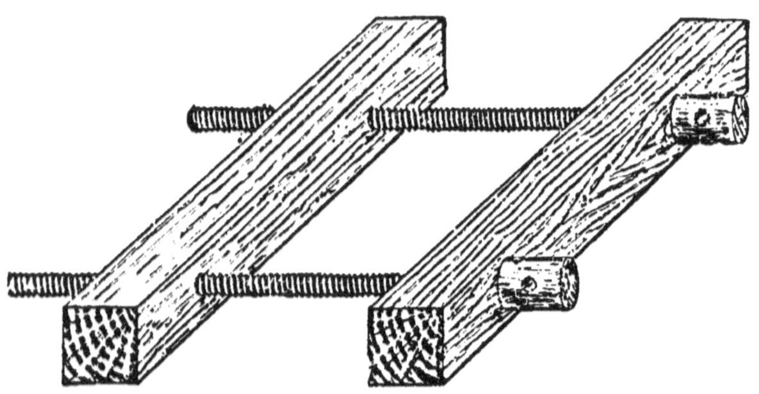

Fig. 64.—Gilder's Press.

as a carpenter's chisel, except that the corners should be rounded a little. Many workers prefer it ground up while soft, so as to cast a "burr" upon the edge, and then hardened; the burr thus produced is used to scrape with, and a scraper thus made will be found to cut very quickly.

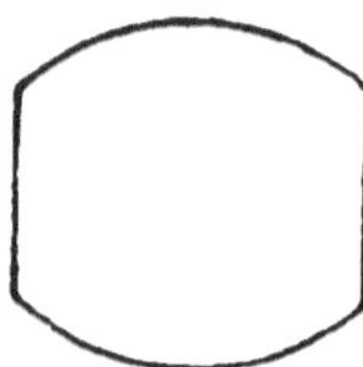

Fig. 65.—Steel Scraper for Book Edges.

The book edge gilder's gold cushion, illustrated by Fig. 66, resembles that used by the painter and decorator, and consists of a flat board measuring about 1 ft. by 9 in. or so, with two or three thicknesses of flannel or printers' press-blanket laid flat upon it, and then covered with a piece of calf-skin, flesh or rough side upwards, nailed down to the edges of the board.

To make a gold cushion, take a piece of wood, size immaterial—12 in. by 6 in. by 1 in. does very well—and lay upon it several sheets of blotting-paper, the bottom one the same size as the wood, the next a shade smaller, the next smaller still, and so on until enough is laid on, and then cover with a piece of calf, the rough side up, and fasten it on by nailing it all round the edge. A slip of stout

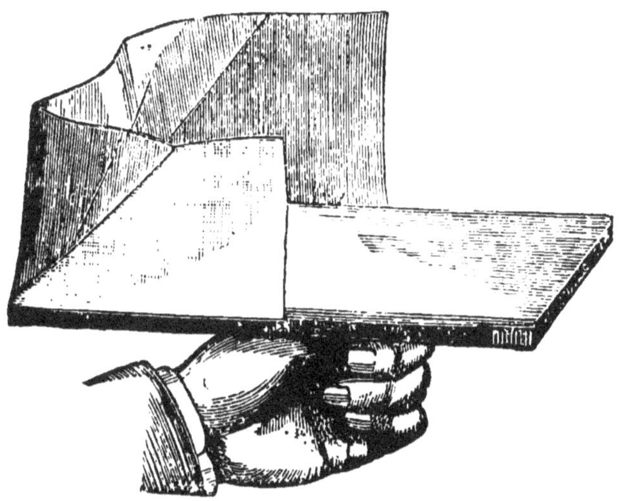

Fig. 66.—Gilder's Cushion.

vellum is generally placed along the edge outside the leather, and nailed through with brass nails with big convex heads, such as upholsterers use for brass-nailing chairs. Decorators and gilders generally protect the cushion with a screen of stout vellum a few inches high, but as the finisher does his work indoors a screen is hardly necessary ; it is, however, shown in the illustration (Fig. 66). Gold cushions can be purchased of any artists' colourman, and of many oilmen. The knife is about

the shape of a palette knife (see Figs. 67 and 68), with
a somewhat rough (but not too rough) cutting edge.
The tip (Fig. 69) is similar to that used by the
decorator and gilder, and consists of a few hairs
of sable secured in a cardboard handle. It is
used for lifting the gold leaf, but many finishers
prefer a bit of cotton-wool or wadding, rendered
slightly greasy by being passed across the forehead.

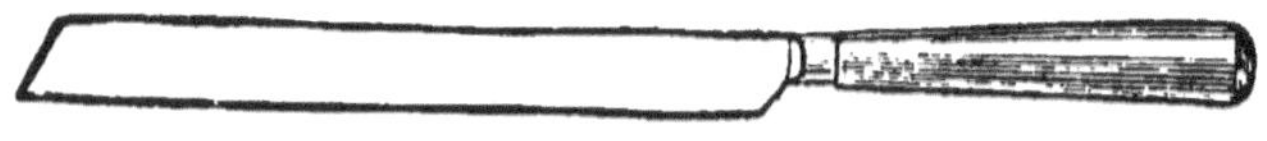

Fig. 67.—Gilder's Knife.

The steel burnisher used is illustrated by Fig.
70 ; it has a wooden handle.

All the gilding done in the finishing of books is
executed with gold leaf. The gold leaf is put up
into small paper books, each containing twenty-five
leaves of gold, and is sold by the hundred leaves
(four books). Gold leaf varies in colour according
to the manner in which the metal is alloyed before
being beaten out. The different tints are deep
gold, ruddy orange, medium gold, pale gold, and
pale lemon. Generally deep gold is preferred by
London binders.

Fig. 68.—Gilder's Knife.

With regard to preparing the edges to receive
the gold, screw the book into the press, with the
edge to be gilt level with the top of the press,
carefully ascertaining that the leaves are quite
level with each other, and then give it a coat of
size. The fore-edges are first dealt with. When
the size is dry, scrape the edge until all irregulari-
ties of the leaves disappear. The scraper, which

should not have a very sharp edge, is held between the thumbs and fingers of both hands in an inclined position, and is worked, with some amount of pressure, along the edges of the book in a direction away from the operator. The scraping is continued until the edges are perfectly level and smooth. To gild edges that have not been properly treated at this stage will simply be a waste of gold.

A little Armenian bole or red ochre, mixed with a little thin glaire, is smeared over the edges with

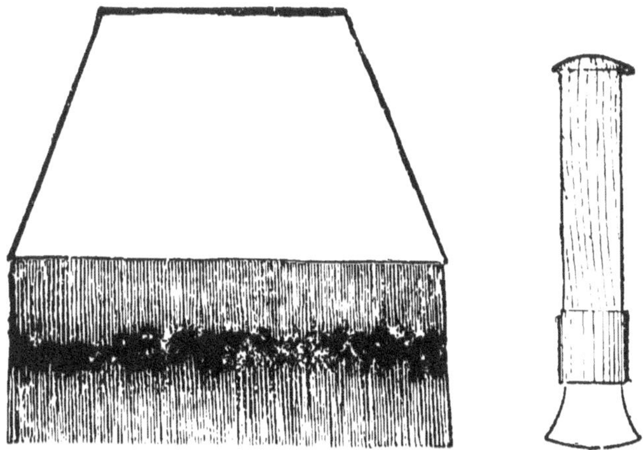

Fig. 69 —Gilder's Tip.   Fig. 70.—Gilder's Burnisher.

a bit of sponge, and then wiped off as clean as possible with a bunch of clean shavings. When dry the edges are burnished. This red ground forms a good foundation for the gilding. The edges are then glaired, and the gold leaf is applied.

An alternative method of treating the edges after scraping is to mix a small portion of size with a little blacklead until they form a paste ; brush some of this on the edge quite evenly, and then brush briskly with a hard brush until dry. If the edges now present an even appearance—no parts being left unblackleaded—apply first a coat of glaire and then the gold-leaf.

Before using the gold cushion its surface should be rubbed over with some Armenian bole or powdered red ochre to prevent the gold adhering to the cushion should the latter be in any way greasy. A leaf of gold is then placed on the cushion and made to lie flat and smooth by blowing gently on the centre of the leaf. The leaf is then cut to the desired size, the edge of the knife being sharp, but not too keen. The tip or cotton-wool is made slightly moist or greasy by drawing it across the forehead; this is done so that the gold-leaf may readily adhere to the tip; or instead cut a piece of writing-paper a little larger than the strips of gold-leaf, and rub it on the hair to make it slightly greasy. There is enough natural grease in the hair of everyone for the purpose mentioned, only the slightest possible amount being needed. The leaf is now picked up by pressing the paper into contact with it, and laid in its place on the book edges.

Suppose it is necessary to use three half-leaves of gold to cover the edge. Lay out two leaves on the cushion and cut both in half with the knife. Supposing pieces of paper to be used, lift up a piece of gold, which then will adhere to the paper. Lay this down, gold upward, and lift the other two pieces in like manner. Now well fill the size brush (a flat camel-brush), and pass it quickly over the edge with one sweep if possible, taking care not to disturb the blacklead; then as quickly as possible lift the gold now on the papers and lay each piece upon the edge. Care must be taken to prevent making holes in the leaf, and the various pieces must overlap but slightly. Holes that have to be patched generally are unsightly, as also are broad overlaps.

If time can be allowed, it is best to protect the

edge from dust and to allow the gold to dry natur-
ally. This may take from three to six hours,
according to the atmosphere of the room in which
the operation is carried on. When dry the gold
must be burnished. The burnisher should be used
in somewhat the same manner as a cobbler bur-
nishes the edges of a boot sole; the main thing is
a fair amount of pressure applied evenly. If the
gold is to be bright, the edges must be rubbed over
with a waxed cloth before burnishing; dull gilt is
produced by keeping a piece of paper between the
gold and the burnisher. The edges are then
papered up until the binding of the book is completed.

The method of burnishing adopted by some
bookbinders is as follows. Before burnishing the
gold is rubbed down with a piece of paper held in
the left hand; then place the paper upon the edge
and rub the burnisher over it. The edge must be
rubbed over with something to prevent the burnisher sticking, beeswax being generally used. A
little is rubbed on the cheek of the press in a convenient position for the right hand, and a piece of
leather or the fleshy part of the hand is rubbed
over the wax, and the edge is rubbed with this.
The burnisher is grasped in the closed hand and
held by the thumb and forefinger; it comes out
between the first and second fingers. The handle
is placed against the shoulder, and this indicates
that considerable pressure is to be used in this
operation. The burnisher is passed forwards and
backwards across the edge. This motion is kept
up until a high degree of polish is obtained, rubbing being done now and again with the wax if
required.

Sometimes, especially in devotional books, em-
blems and devices are painted in water-colours on
the gilt fore-edges. Another plan, effective but
expensive, and therefore seldom resorted to, is to

fan out the edges, and paint on them in water-colours a landscape, figures, or appropriate floral or other patterns and devices. The book is then gilded on the edges in the usual manner. A specimen can be seen in the Guildhall Library, London, E.C.

The "red under gold" effect is produced by reddening the edges first. Other colours are often used, such as "green under gold," etc., but the method is the same in all cases. For red, get a sufficient quantity of vermilion (a dry colour in powder), place it on a stone slab, mix it into a paste with water, and with a stone muller grind it until it is very fine and smooth. Then mix it in a cup with glaire thin enough to be applied with a sponge. This done, take the book (which must be cut on all edges) and place it on the bench, opening it from about the middle so that the same number of leaves may lie to right and left. Put a backing board on the right-hand side of the open leaves flush with the edge, press it down tightly with the left hand, and with a sponge dipped in the colour put an even coating over this part of the book edge. By this method the sides of the edges of the book are coloured and will always show when the book is open, which is the effect desired. Then turn the book round and treat the left-hand side in the same manner, and when dry close the book, turn it round, open again, and colour the other side of the edges. This completes the fore-edge of the book. The ends will be more difficult to manipulate. With the book flat on the bench and with the fore-edge towards the operator, take the right-hand corner of the book between the thumb and finger of the right hand and move it towards the left, pushing the top part of the book backwards, and when in this position hold it so with the left hand. Then put the backing board on as before and colour this edge. Turn the book

over and repeat the moving process in the opposite direction and again apply the colour.   The
other end is treated in the same way.   When
the edges are dry, the book is put into the press
and the ordinary gilding operations are proceeded
with.

CHAPTER XII.

SPRINKLING AND TREE MARBLING BOOK COVERS.

THE covers of books bound in plain uncoloured calf or sheepskin are sometimes sprinkled in order to relieve the monotony of a plain unornamented surface. But the custom is not so common now as it was fifty or more years ago. Very pretty effects can, however, be produced in this way. The materials and the methods employed are the same as adopted for sprinkling book edges.

Sprinkling on panels, as illustrated by Fig. 71 (see opposite page), is a style of ornamentation that may be made very effective. By calling the work a kind of stencilling, the manner of doing it is explained. Such panels, borders, or other patterns are afterwards blind-tooled by the finisher.

The marbling of the covers of leather-bound books is produced by the application of solutions of pearlash and green copperas. The book is supported open as for sprinkling. The operator dips into clean water a coarse brush or a bundle of feathers tied together, and throws some large drops of water on the book. As the covers are extended in a slanting position, these drops of water run down and form irregular rivulets. A smaller brush is then dipped into a strong solution of pearlash (potash), with which the cover of the book is lightly sprinkled, and lastly a solution of green copperas is added with a still smaller brush. All this is done so quickly that the drops of water trickling down carry with them some of each of these solutions and stain the leather a rich brown (pearlash) and black (copperas). The cover is then well sponged with clean water.

Tree marbling is formed on calf-bound books in much the same manner as ordinary sprinkling, except that the boards are bent outwards to allow the water and colours to run to the centre and produce what seem to be the branches of trees. The name is also given to such processes as endeavour to imitate the grain of wood. As the success of the processes often depends on the quickness with which they are executed, it is important that

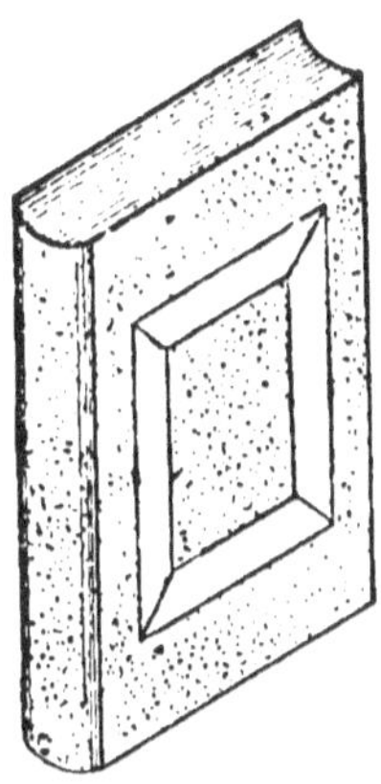

Fig. 71.—Sprinkling on Panels.

the colours, sponges, brushes, etc., are easy of access.

For this work the books are bound with what is termed fair calf, this being leather which has not been dyed. First the books must be carefully washed with paste water containing a little salts of tartar and then left to dry. Some workers also coat them with glaire, but this, whilst allowing the colours to flow freely, has a tendency to prevent them striking in where wanted. When thoroughly dry the volume is placed between marbling rods, the sides of the book hanging over with the leaves between the rods as shown in Fig. 72.

The rods should slope so as to allow the water to run gradually towards the bottom of the book, and if the back is to be left plain it must be covered with a piece of millboard or strawboard shaped to suit.

To avoid the scum which is caused by the beating of the brushes over the colours, it is better to rub the ends of the bristles on the palm of the hand, on which a little olive oil has been spread. The brushes should be such as are used for sprinkling edges, and should be bound with iron rings. A bunch of quills or birch rods will also be required for throwing on the water.

For ordinary work, with the book on the rods, throw on the water in large drops until these unite. Then a number of fine streaks are produced by throwing colour evenly over the entire cover, using a brush charged with brown liquid and beaten on the press-pin as when sprinkling edges. Afterwards the black liquid must be similarly thrown over. This must be done quickly; in fact, while the water continues to run.

Marbling water should be soft, and should have added to it a few drops of salts of tartar. Brown colour is prepared by dissolving $\frac{1}{4}$ lb. of salts of tartar in 1 quart of water. For black colour, dissolve $\frac{1}{2}$ lb. of green copperas in 2 quarts of water. A good blue colour may be prepared by mixing 1 oz. of powdered indigo with 2 oz. of oil of vitriol and letting it stand for twenty-four hours and then adding 12 oz. of pure water. One of the best yellow colours is prepared from hay saffron. Put a small quantity in a cup or similar vessel, fill up with water, and set beside a hot stove and allow to infuse. The quantities are immaterial, as the liquid can be made of whatever strength desired by simply adding water to the stock solution, which should be kept in a bottle. For green colour, liquid blue and yellow mixed will suit all purposes. For red colour, boil $\frac{1}{2}$ lb. of Brazil wood and 8 gr. of nutgalls, both powdered, in 3 pints of water; let it boil for a considerable time until it is reduced about one-third, and then add 1 oz. each of powdered alum and sal-ammoniac, and when dissolved strain through a sieve. This must always be used warm. Orange colour is produced from red and yellow liquid.

These colours should all be kept in well-corked bottles and in a dark place, if possible. They can be used full strength or diluted with water if desired.

In addition, an acid of some kind is necessary for the work. The safest to use is oxalic acid, cf

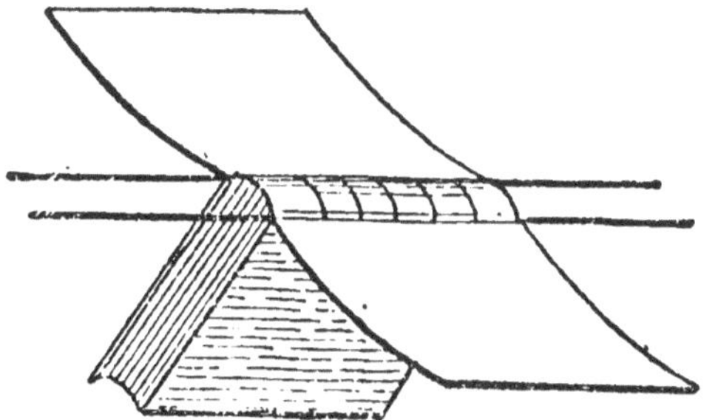

Fig. 72.—Book between Marbling Rods.

which a saturated solution should be kept in use; a few drops only should be added to the water. The proportion should not exceed one of acid in twenty of water, otherwise the leather may be corroded or destroyed.

For walnut effect, throw on the water in large spots and then quickly sprinkle with brown first, and afterwards with black. For cedar, sprinkle as for walnut, and, before the cover is perfectly dry, in various places on the cover daub lightly with an open-holed sponge dipped in orange so as to form a cloud effect. When this is dry, apply red as nearly as possible on the same places, and when perfectly dry give the whole two or three coats of yellow, taking care that each coat penetrates evenly into the leather. For mahogany, act as for walnut, but sprinkle the black more boldly, and, when the work is dry, give two or three coats of red. For box, the boards must be bent in five or six different places ; then proceed as for walnut. After the work is perfectly dry, throw water in large drops and sprinkle small spots with weak blue ; when the work is dry, apply red with a sponge as directed for the cedar. Finally, when dry give two or three coats of orange.

CHAPTER XIII.

LETTERING, GILDING, AND FINISHING BOOK COVERS.

FINISHING includes all the methods employed for decorating the cover of a book. The most usual form of decoration consists in impressing on the book cover, in leaf metal (gold, silver, or other suitable metal), various designs of an ornamental character. A similar impressed design, with the metal leaf omitted (called blind work), is also employed. Book covers are also decorated with super-imposed metal ornaments, which are riveted on. Ivory and other materials are also employed for purposes of ornamentation; but the most usual form of decoration is by gilding and blind work. The finishing of leather books is imitated in cloth. In the former, all the decoration is done by the hand of the workman, the design being worked out or built up bit by bit; in the latter, the ornamented cover is produced in a mechanical manner by printing from an engraved block. The comparing together of two ornamented books, one cloth and one leather, will enable even a superficial observer to see the difference in the style of decoration, and will give some idea, too, of the great number and the variety of the tools required by the finisher. The more necessary of these numerous tools are described below.

The finishing press is a small screw press (Fig. 73), smaller and less powerful than the ordinary lying-press; it stands on the bench or counter at which the operator works.

The finishing stove is used for heating the tools, and generally is a specially contrived gas stove. Fig. 74 shows a small one that can be stood on the

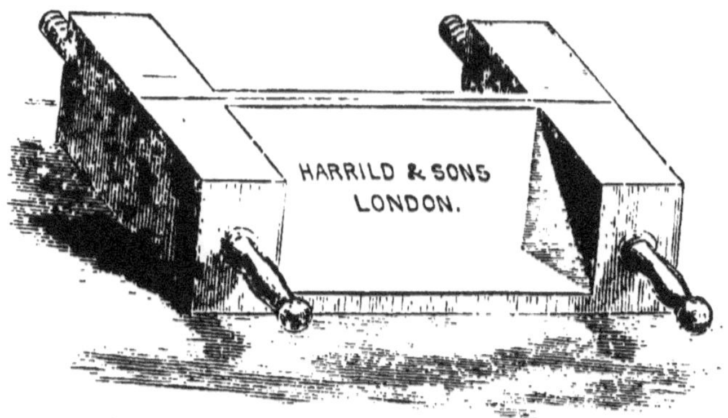

Fig. 73

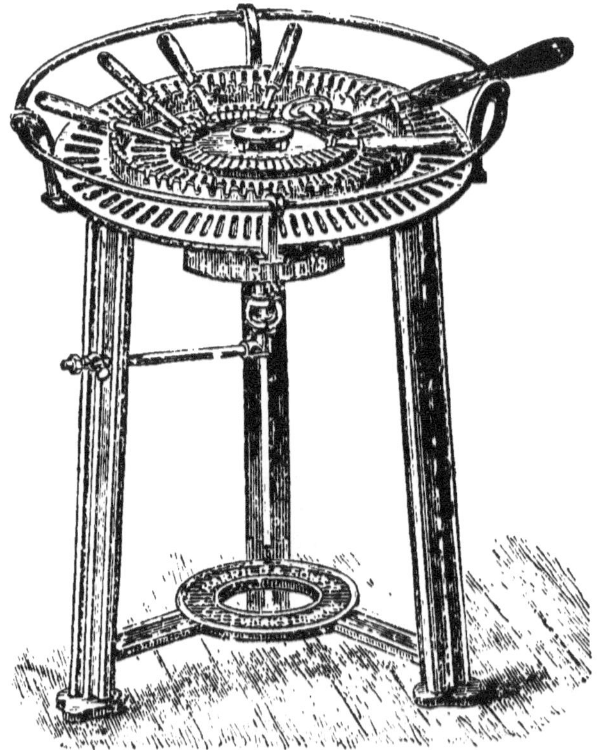

Fig. 74

Fig. 73.—Finisher's Press.   Fig. 74.—Finisher's Stove.

work-bench or on a tall tripod. An ordinary oil stove can, of course, be used if gas is not available.

The fillet (Fig. 75) is used for gilding plain lines on the backs of books. The tool is simply a small,

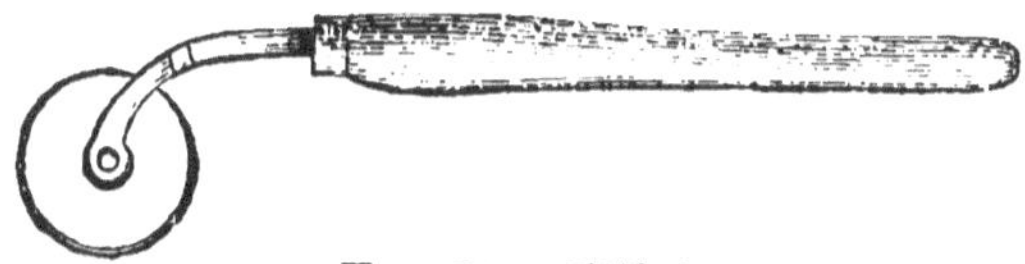

Fig. 75.—Fillet

freely revolving brass wheel mounted in an iron carriage that is fixed in a strong wooden handle.

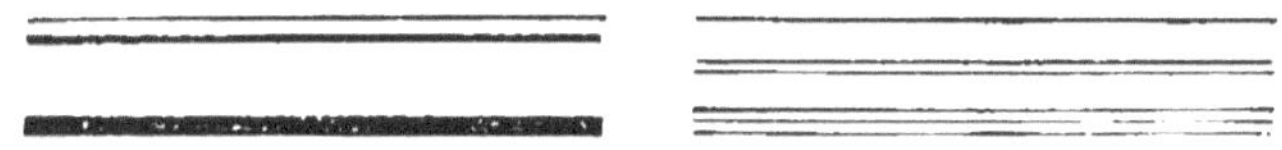

Fig. 76.—Lines made with Fillets.

Fillets of various kinds are made; they are known as thin, thick, extra thick, thick and thin, etc., and

Fig. 77.—Line made with Pallet.

one-, two-, and three-line fillets. A few examples of the lines (Figs. 76 and 77) produced by different

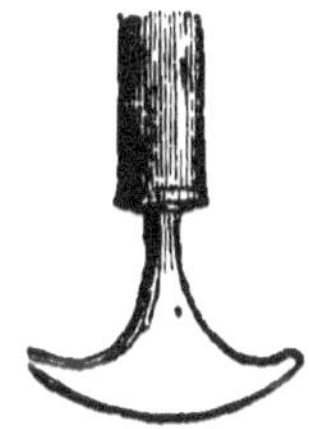

Fig. 78.—Pallet.

fillets will also illustrate the manner in which the tool is employed.

The roll is also a brass wheel, similar to a fillet, but broader in the rim. Instead, however, of tracing lines, the roll reproduces any ornamental designs that have been cut upon its surface by the bookbinder's tool cutter.

The general form of pallets, which are of various

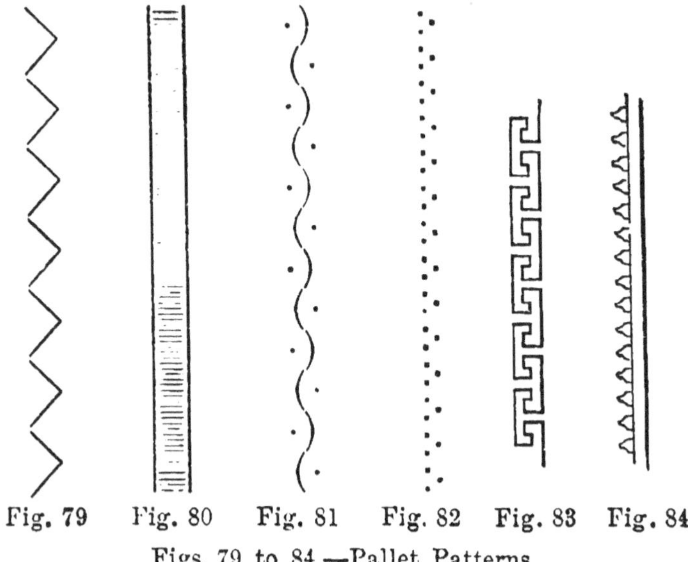

Fig. 79 Fig. 80 Fig. 81 Fig. 82 Fig. 83 Fig. 84

Figs. 79 to 84.—Pallet Patterns.

sizes, is shown by Fig. 78. The shape of the tool suggests the manner of using it. The variety of patterns that may be cut upon pallets is infinite, from

Fig. 85.—Line Tools.

the most simple zig-zag to a broad belt of flowers and leaves. Figs. 79 to 84 show simple but useful patterns.

Line tools are shaped something like pallets, but

are made in sets of ten or a dozen tools of various lengths. Specimens of the lines produced by them are shown by Figs. 85 to 87.

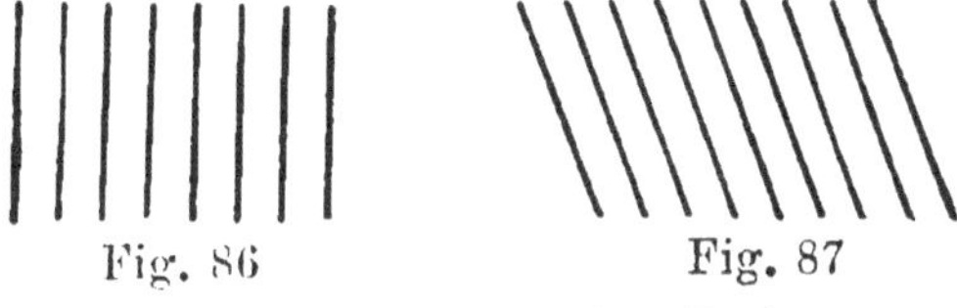

Fig. 86   Fig. 87

Figs. 86 and 87.—Line Tools.

Gouges (Figs. 88 and 89) are curved line tools. They are made in sets, and also in various curvatures, from a quarter-circle to a complete circle.

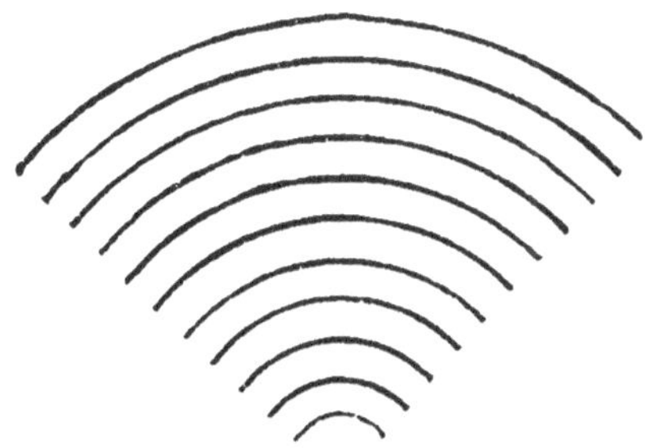

Fig. 88.—Lines made with Gouges

These tools are of great use in patterns made by the combination of straight lines and curves.

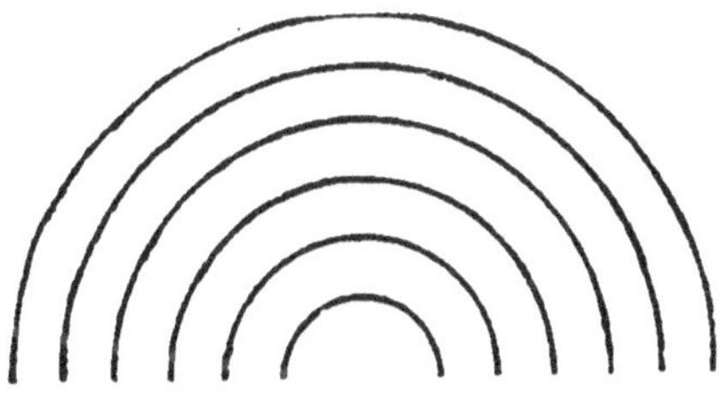

Fig. 89.—Lines made with Gouges.

Drop tools, flowers, and other ornamental separate tools are used in great variety. In an elaborate design, every ornament may require a separate tool, and the binder's tool cutter is always at work. Fig. 90 is an example of a small finishing tool.

The ends of tools for producing corners and centres are shown in Figs. 91 to 94, and being repeat tools, four impressions of each will produce a centre. Other simple designs are shown by Figs. 95 to 98.

To show how the above tools are used on the

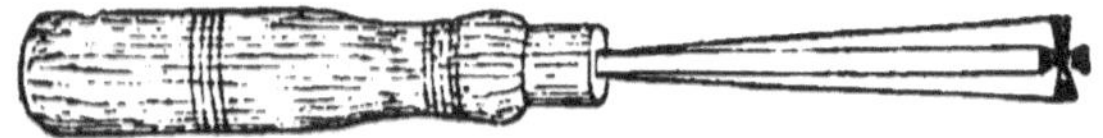

Fig. 90.—Small Finishing Tool.

covers of books is unnecessary, when so many examples can be seen in the shop windows of high-class booksellers and in bookbinders' show-cases. One example, however, of a book back may be given (Fig. 99), and from it will be seen how it is possible to produce elaborate effects by combinations of simple ornaments.

Finishing requires not only careful attention in every detail, but a considerable amount of taste and

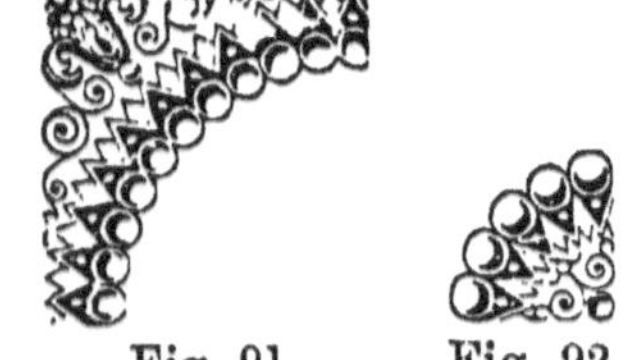

Fig. 91

Fig. 92   Fig. 93

Fig. 94

Figs. 91 to 94.—Corner Patterns, Four of each making Centre Patterns.

ability ; taste to form a true estimate of what will harmonise with the nature of the work and add to the beauty of the binding, and ability to execute the designs.

According to the custom of the shop (see p. 64), the finisher's first business may be to examine the book critically, and if he finds any defects in the

Fig. 95

Fig. 96

Fig. 97

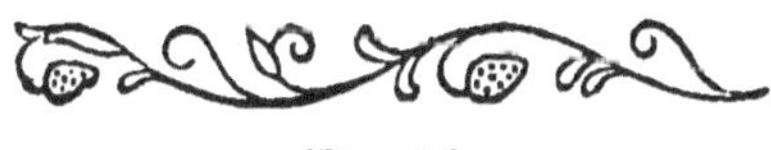

Fig. 98

Figs. 95 to 98.—Cover Ornaments. Fig. 99.—Finished
Back of Book.

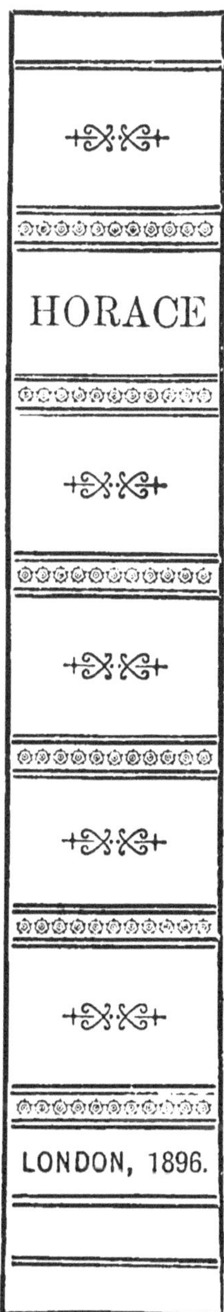

Fig. 99

forwarding he should point them out. With a band-stick (a piece of hard wood about 10 in. by 1 in. by ½ in. planed square) the leather is rubbed close into the sides of the bands, providing there are bands. If the book is bound in calf, a small piece of thin leather of a colour harmonising with the colour of the cover is cut out, pared neatly, and pasted on where the title is to appear (see p. 62).

Morocco and roan binding seldom have coloured titles, so they are not " pieced," as it is termed.

The book should next be trimmed, that is, all inequalities left by the forwarder in the cover should be pared evenly by the finisher. Backs, corners, sides, and insides should be treated in this manner, for a bad appearance is given to a finished book by lumps of leather showing beneath the cloth or paper of the sides or insides. The board should be opened, one of the end papers torn out (back and front) and laid aside for lining the boards after-wards and the joints scraped to take away any little pieces of paste or glue that may have lodged there. The end paper which is to be pasted to the board should be trimmed at the sides, so that it will be at equal distances all round from the edge of the board. Attention to these little matters, although they may seem trivial, will go a long way in adding to the beauty of the finished volume. But it may be that all the finisher will be required to do is to proceed at once with the finishing directly he re-ceives the book.

All leather-bound books are washed with paste-water, that is, clear water with a little paste mixed in it. This replaces, or in some cases supplements, the vellum size used formerly.

Calf, because of its great porosity, requires to be well rubbed with paste before washing. Paste the back with the brush, and rub the paste well into the leather with the folder, taking care not to rub too hard. Sometimes a little oxalic acid is added to the paste-water, and this helps to clear the lighter colours of leather. Discretion will have to be used in this matter, as the acid will destroy some colours.

For lettering the backs of books, at one time each letter of the alphabet was mounted as a separate tool, and this plan still occasionally is met with.

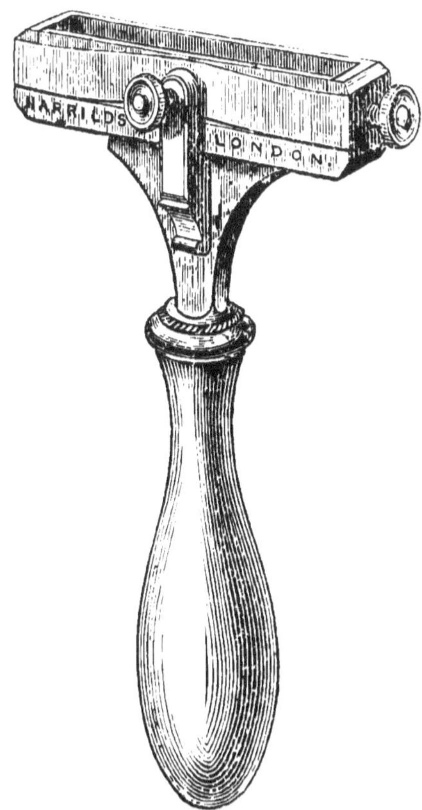

Fig. 100.—Letter Holder.

The modern plan is to cut the letters in brass type and use them in a typeholder. The ordinary types employed in printing are also sometimes used. They are arranged in a holder (Fig. 100), and may be spaced out to fill the width of the back or put close together, as may be found necessary.

Small implements and utensils also are necessary. An earthenware pipkin, glazed inside, is required for boiling the size. It should be provided with a flat tin lid. An instrument called the " devil " (Fig. 101) is used in preparing the glaire, which can be kept in any small earthenware vessel ; the devil consists of two pieces of quill fastened as shown to a long stick like a penholder. It is used like an egg whisk. Two polishers used for polishing and smoothing the back and sides of the book after finishing are shown in Figs. 102 and 103. Fig. 102 is the polisher generally preferred by London binders, and is very useful

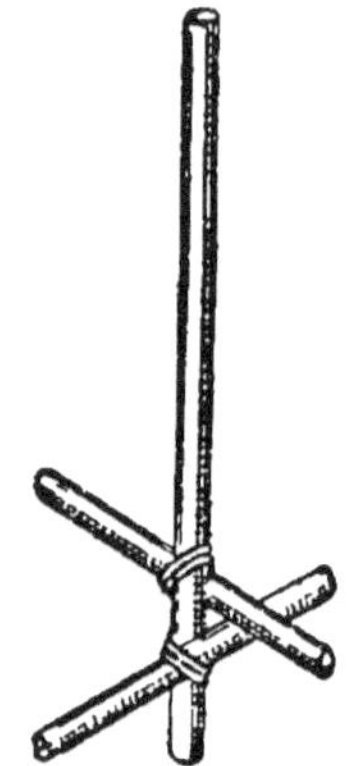

Fig. 101.—Devil for Preparing Glaire.

for working close to the bands, but the one shown by Fig. 103 is very good for the sides of whole-calf volumes. Some pieces of sponge, two or three camel-hair pencils, a gold rag, several small pieces of flannel, and a bit of good raw rubber are also required. The materials used by the finisher are few, and, with the exception of gold leaf, are of little value.

Finishers' size is made from waste slips of vellum. which are cut up very small, put with sufficient water into a clean pipkin, and allowed to boil gently. It will not keep long, and fresh size should be made often.

Glaire is made by breaking the white of a fresh egg into a tea-cup, carefully excluding the yolk,

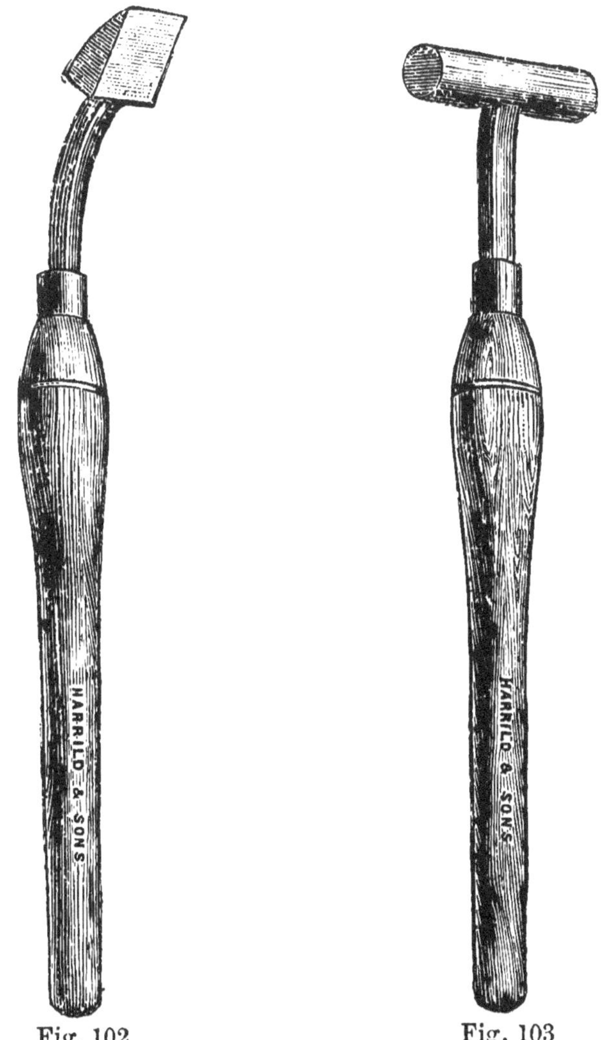

Fig. 102   Fig. 103

Figs. 102 and 103.—Polishers.

adding water until the cup is about half full, beating well together, and adding a pinch of salt as a preservative. This having been allowed to stand for a few hours, is carefully strained through a piece of old linen and bottled for use. No particle of the yolk should be mixed with the white. A usual method of making the glaire is by rolling the devil with a rapid motion between the palms of the hands, the quills being in the albumen. When all the albumen has been beaten to froth it is put aside to settle, and the result is glaire. The original white of eggs is ropy and gelatinous, but the frothing up makes it as thin and fluent as water. Another method is to place the whites of two or three eggs in a cup, and add a small quantity of vinegar and a pinch of salt, beating the whole well together. At the end of a minute or two remove the froth from the top and place the preparation in a bottle.

The glaire, when ready, is applied all over the cover of the book with a small sponge. When the first coat is thoroughly dry give it another.

The back or side of the book on which the gold is to be affixed must be slightly greased after the application of the last coat of glaire. Finishers differ somewhat as to the material to be employed. Olive oil is used by, perhaps, most workmen ; lard, or composite, or some kind of palm-oil candle is also used. But the quantity required is so small that any tolerably pure fatty or oily substance will do.

Sometimes, in order to add to the glossy appearance of calf backs, and also in some degree to serve as a preservative coating, some kind of fine spirit varnish is applied to the leather. The varnish should be of the best quality, both as regards the spirit used as a solvent, and the copal, mastic, or other gum dissolved in it.

Suppose, as a sufficiently typical example, that the finisher is about to deal with a batch of from twelve to twenty half-calf books. The first operation is to paste-wash the leather. A small quantity of thick paste is applied to the back of the book, and rubbed up and down the back with a folding-stick.

This forces the paste into and fills up the small pores of the leather, and thus forms a foundation for the succeeding operations. The paste is then washed off the back with a sponge and clean water, the sides of the back and the corners being also wiped over with the pasty water in the sponge. When dry, the leather is sponged over with warm size, and, when the size is dry, the glaire is applied with a bit of sponge (kept specially for that purpose), or with a camel-hair pencil.

The best procedure for ordinary half-calf work (or for whole calf where there is to be no finishing on the sides) is, for the first application, to go over all the leather with the glaire. When this coating is dry, a second coat is applied, this time to the back only. A third coating can be given, either to the entire back, as in the previous application, or merely across the lettering piece. When the backs of the books are sufficiently dry, a piece of cotton-wool to which the least touch of oil or lard has been applied is passed rapidly over all the surface that is to be gilded. The strips of leaf are lifted to the place that is to be gilded either with the tip or with a bit of cotton-wool, the slight oiling the cover has received causing the leaf instantly to adhere where it is placed.

The books are now ready for the next stage. It should be remarked here, however, that until the amateur has acquired some experience, he will do well to mark lightly on the back or cover, as the case may be, with a folder, the positions the ornaments and lettering are to occupy. The advisability of working from a sketch plan will also be evident. The good appearance of even excellent ornamentation on a book cover, as elsewhere, will be marred and probably spoilt if the arrangement is not symmetrical.

Pressure with hot tools causes the gold leaf to adhere to the leather, and reproduces at the same time the pattern engraved on the tool. The heat

of the tool is tested with a drop of water, which, if
the tool is hot enough, should evaporate quickly
without hissing; if the water hisses, the tool is too
hot.

Suppose a volume to be screwed up in the finishing press (Fig. 73, p. 116), which is lying on the bench
in front of the worker, the head of the book being
towards the right hand; the heated fillet is taken
from the stove, and the edge of the fillet, which
must be perfectly clean and bright, is drawn quickly
over the palm of the left hand to aid the adhesion
of the gold. The fillet is then rolled carefully over
the slips of gold leaf, which will adhere to the fillet

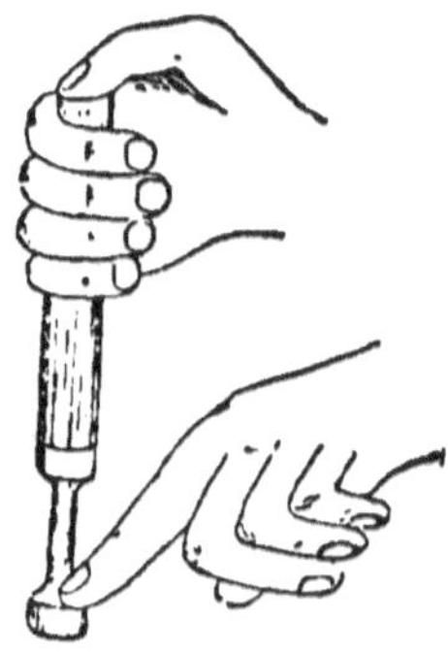

Fig. 104.—Method of Holding Lettering Tool.

till its periphery is covered. Then turning to the
book, hold the bottom of the handle of the fillet with
the right hand, allow the upper part of the handle to
rest against the right shoulder, and roll the fillet
over the back of the book at the places marked for
the bands. Having thus filleted the back seven
times (if an octavo), the finisher shifts the press so
that the tail of the book is towards him, raises the
head of the book somewhat higher than the tail, so
that the back is rather inclined, and then proceeds
to apply the lettering upon the lettering piece, previously covered with a piece of gold leaf as
described.

If lettering is done with the separate handled letters, great care will be required to keep the line straight and the letters equidistant. It is best to stamp first the central letter of the title, and then to add the others on each side. Thus, in lettering **HOMER**, the **M** would be first applied, then **O** and **E**, and lastly **H** and **R**. The full title screwed up in a typeholder is more easily applied, but even by this method considerable care is required. Centre

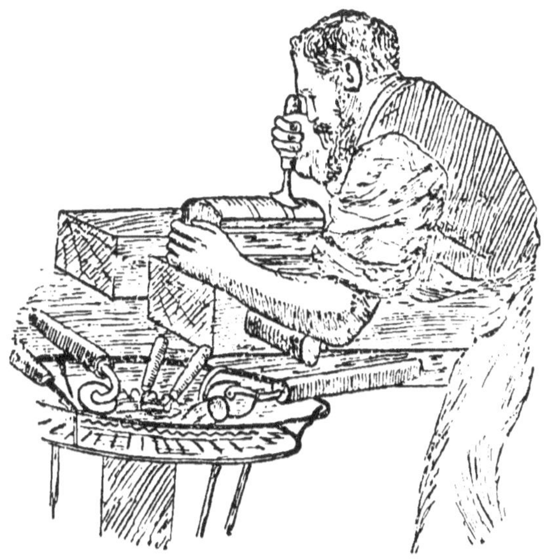

Fig. 105.—Method of Applying Pallet.

ornaments, corners, pallets, and, in fact, all other tools necessary for the production of half-gilt or full-gilt backs, are worked in a similar manner. In placing the smaller tools the binder holds the upper part of the handle in the right hand and guides the end with the thumb, as shown at Fig. 104. The pallets are worked carefully across the backs. Sometimes the finisher works a light blind impression of the tool first to guide him, then lays on the gold leaf, and applies the heated tool again (see Fig. 105).

The following instruction on lettering is specially

applicable to the amateur who possesses but very few appliances. As in working with single letters it is very difficult to keep them even, both as regards the straightness of the lines and the distance of one letter from another, the amateur may find very useful a small and inexpensive apparatus which he can make easily for himself. The method is illustrated by Fig. 106, where A is a piece of flat wood,

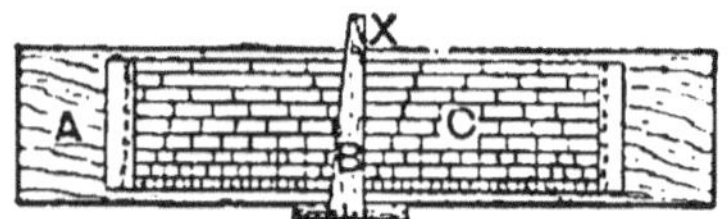

Fig. 106.—Method of Spacing Letters.

¼ in. thick, 1¼ in. wide, and about 6 in. long ; B is a small T-square with one edge tapered off, as shown ; C is a paper scale, marked out as in Fig. 107, and pasted or glued on. Fig. 107 is reproduced full size. The exactness with which the letters can be placed in position by means of this appliance will amply repay the time taken in making it.

The proper type may be procured from any of

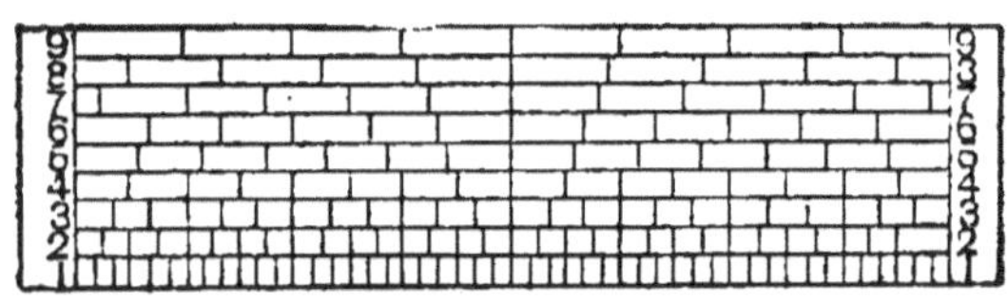

Fig. 107.—Scale for Spacing Letters.

the firms who deal in bookbinder's tools ; but where economy is an important object, the local printer would probably supply, at small cost, a set of printing types, which, provided that care be taken not to break them by rough usage, nor to melt them by overheating, will be found to serve the purpose just as well as brass types.

A holder for single letters can be made by the worker. Get a piece of iron rod, $\frac{3}{8}$ in. or $\frac{1}{2}$ in. in diameter, and about 3 in. or 4 in. long, and file it to the shape shown at A (Fig. 108). Make a piece of the same shape as B, and see that when A and B are placed together they form a round rod, that is, B simply fills up A where it has been filed away. With a small square file reduce B to the shape indicated at E, and then with a small sharp chisel cut A in the same manner about $\frac{7}{8}$ in. up. When A and B are placed together they form a square, which is for the purpose of holding the letter to be used. Now make a small screw with head—about No. 10 B.W.G.—and having done this, drill a hole through A, $\frac{3}{4}$ in. from the end, to allow the screw to drop through ; continue it through B, but make it smaller

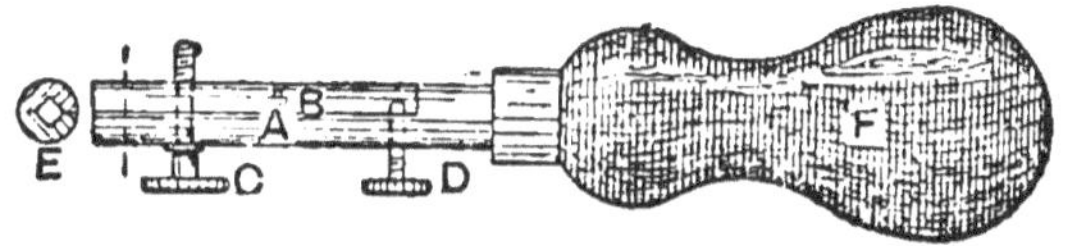

Fig. 108.—Type Holder.

than the hole in A, because, whilst the hole in A allows the screw to drop through, that in B requires to be tapped. Take care at this point—A is clean through, B is tapped. The screw D should be made a little shorter than C, but of the same diameter. A hole should be drilled for the screw to pass through, as shown ; but in this case the hole in A is tapped. Continue the hole into B, but not quite through it, and then enlarge the hole until the screw will drop into it. It has now only to be driven into a haft, when it will be ready for use.

The method of using this holder is as follows : Unscrew the knob C until the letter to be used will drop into the square, and then screw in D until it forms a pivot for B to work upon. It will not be necessary for D to be moved, except when a different size of letter is to be used ; simply tightening C will cause it to grip the letter, and a slight turn back will allow the latter to fall out. The typeholder and the guide will ensure perfectly straight lines and equal spaces.

The gold leaf can be bought at 1s. 1½d. or 1s. 3d. per book. Dutch metal is the best imitation, but no matter how good the imitation, time will destroy, more or less slowly but very surely, the lustre of the metal, and finally turn it black. When it is considered how small a quantity is used at a time, it is clear that the purchase of inferior leaf is inadvisable.

In arranging the title the object aimed at is to enable the book to be found at a glance. If the title occupies two lines, the first line may be in larger type than the second; if three lines, the first should be largest and boldest, the second smallest, and the third of a size midway between the first and second; but a great number of modern books have their two- and three-line titles all in one size type. Suppose that the title shown in Fig. 109 is to be printed. If it is set out as shown, and the year put about two-thirds down, the result will be as effective as a much more elaborate arrangement.

Take the volume and screw it in the press, with the back of the book level with the top of the press. Place the ruler (Fig. 106) across the book, and, by means of two pins, fix it in position to the upper edges of the press. The best size scale for the word WORK will be that marked No. 4. A good bold type will be best for this. Lay it on the stove, in the oven, or in front of the fire to get hot (being careful, if the type is of ordinary type-metal, that it does not reach melting-point). With a small sponge, damp the space to which the letters are to be applied, and lay on a piece of gold leaf large enough to cover the letters. Take up the letter W, fix it in the holder, and see that it is of about the same heat as a sad-iron when in use. Now place the T-square across the first mark to be used on scale 4, put the heated letter into the corner formed by the ruler and square, marked x on Fig. 106, and press it firmly on to the gold leaf, keeping it on for a few moments. Put the W aside and fix the O in the holder, move the square to the next mark on the scale, and repeat the operation as before, and so on, till all the lettering is done. Now move the ruler a little lower down and print in " Vol. 24." Scale No. 3 will do for this, using smaller type.

Fig. 109.—Back of Book.

The ruler should now be moved lower down the book, to the position before indicated, and the year, " 1902," printed. The superfluous gold leaf is wiped off with a greased sponge, when the letters should stand revealed, clear and perfect. It will be noticed that, although lines have been represented above and below the title, no mention has been made of them. This is a simple matter. Where the type is procured, lines, technically termed "rules," of various kinds can be got, or they can easily be made from scraps of sheet brass, and then they can be used in the same manner as the type. Or together with the various ornaments, etc., so often seen on books, they can be added by means of the tools already illustrated in this chapter.

In shops where a great deal of lettering and ornamenting has to be done, a lettering press (Fig. 110) is used. The lettering or ornament is attached to the platen of the press, which is heated by gas, and is brought down forcibly by working the handle, somewhat after the manner of a hand printing press.

The sides of whole-bound calf books may either be left plain and polished or grained with a gold roll run around the sides of the boards, the edges, and the inside of the squares. These places can be specially re-glaired. The rolls are used on the side in the same manner as described for the fillet.

In what is termed "antique" work the calf is not glaired all over, but is left dull. The lettering piece is glaired, and also the bands if the latter are to receive any gilding. The centre ornament, generally a leaf, acorn, or Maltese cross, is worked blind, the place glaired with a camel-hair pencil, and the hot tool worked on it again, the superfluous gold being rubbed off.

Sizing may be omitted for morocco and goatskin, glaire being applied only to those portions that are to be gilded. Roan may be glaired all over the back, and one coating should be sufficient. For inlaid Grolier patterns or the sides of calf or morocco books, the various line tools, gouges, etc., may be worked blind, the impressions then glaired with the camel-hair pencil, slightly oiled, the gold leaf laid on, and the hot tools carefully worked again. Care should be taken to keep the pressure used as nearly equal everywhere as possible, as nothing looks worse in a design than very deep impressions at some places and very slight ones at others. In no case must the tool be heated too much, or it will burn the leather and perhaps cut right through. Sometimes, although not often, the sides of calf- or morocco-bound volumes are decorated with large and special designs, stamped on by the arming press.

The ornamentation of book covers by gold block-

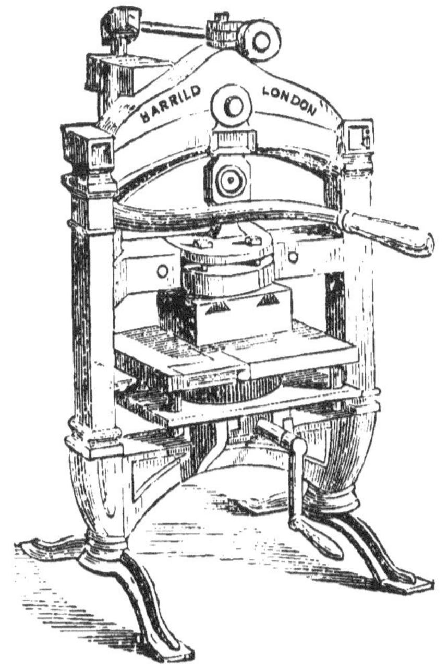

Fig. 110.—Lettering Press.

ing them with fancy designs and ornaments will now be treated in detail. The iron blocking presses (Fig. 110) necessary for gold blocking are generally on one principle, and the chief parts of each are a heater box, a blocking plate, and a bed. Hand presses are set in motion by a lever, and in steam presses by a pulley driven by belt.

The heater box (Fig. 111) is simply a mass of metal pierced with two or more holes, in which lie the atmospheric gas burners which give the required heat. The bottom of this box is planed level and a slot is cut in its entire length. This slot holds the blocking plate (Fig. 112), a flat iron plate, perfectly smooth on both sides. On the upper side is screwed a bar shaped to fit in the slot in the heater box. A lug in front is pierced with a hole, through which a thumbscrew passes to the heater box to keep the plate in position. The bed is also a flat plate provided with gauges at right angles to each other.

An arrangement is provided underneath the bed for raising or lowering it as desired according to the thickness of the work in hand, or for giving more or less pressure suitable to the various blocks or materials to be dealt with from time to time.

Blocks or stamps are for the most part cut in brass, and when new are generally about $\frac{1}{4}$ in. thick; they are also made by the electrotyping process, and often ordinary stereotype blocks are used.

A block for a book cover or the lid of a box, etc., may be made up of several pieces. For instance, there may be four pieces of line for the outer border, four pieces with a floral or other pattern, four corner pieces to match, a lettering piece, and a crest or monogram for the centre. These pieces are mounted together neatly so that they fit or cover the desired space as Figs. 112 and 113, which are the halves of an album cover design registered by Messrs. De la Rue and Co., London; the width as illustrated is less in proportion to the height than it should be, owing to a portion of the design being cut out to accommodate it to these pages. Figs. 115 to 118 represent the various parts used, the design being completed with a few lines.

Before beginning work the blocking press must be heated, the gas in the heater box being lighted some hours in advance. Take a piece of brown paper somewhat larger than the block; it must be of good quality, that known as " casing " being very serviceable. On it draw two lines at right angles to each other near the edges; then glue one of the pieces of the broad and narrow line. A convenient method of applying the glue is to use a lump of dry glue and, having heated the piece of line, rub the glue over it; the heat will of course melt the glue and the fingers will be kept clean. Place the line on the paper carefully close to the pencil line, glue another piece, and place it in the same manner against the other line, taking care that the corner is properly formed. Glue the other two pieces in like manner, one after the other, and lay them upon

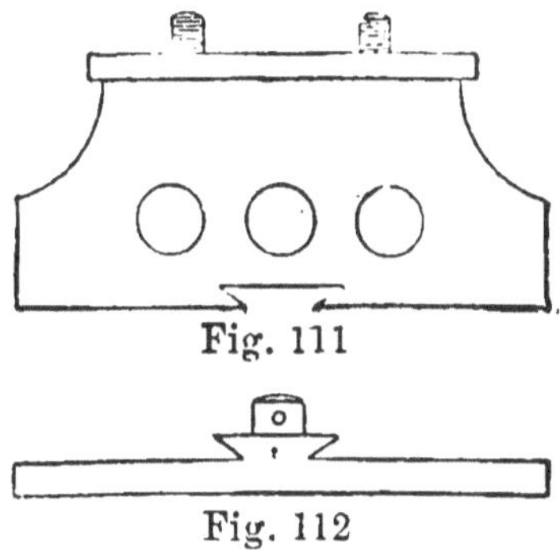

Fig. 111

Fig. 112

Fig. 111.—Heater Box.   Fig. 112.—Blocking Plate.

the paper; attention must be given specially to the corners, and if the pieces have been cut and mitred properly a perfect rectangular border will be the result. While this is lying on the bench, place over it a piece of strawboard, larger of course than the space occupied by the lines. Draw the whole carefully off the bench on to the flat hand and turn it over sharply so as to have the board underneath; then push it carefully on the bed of the press as near the centre as can be judged by the eye and pull down the lever, causing the blocking plate to press upon it. The heat of this plate will first melt the glue and afterwards dry it, thus causing the lines to adhere to the brown paper. After having been

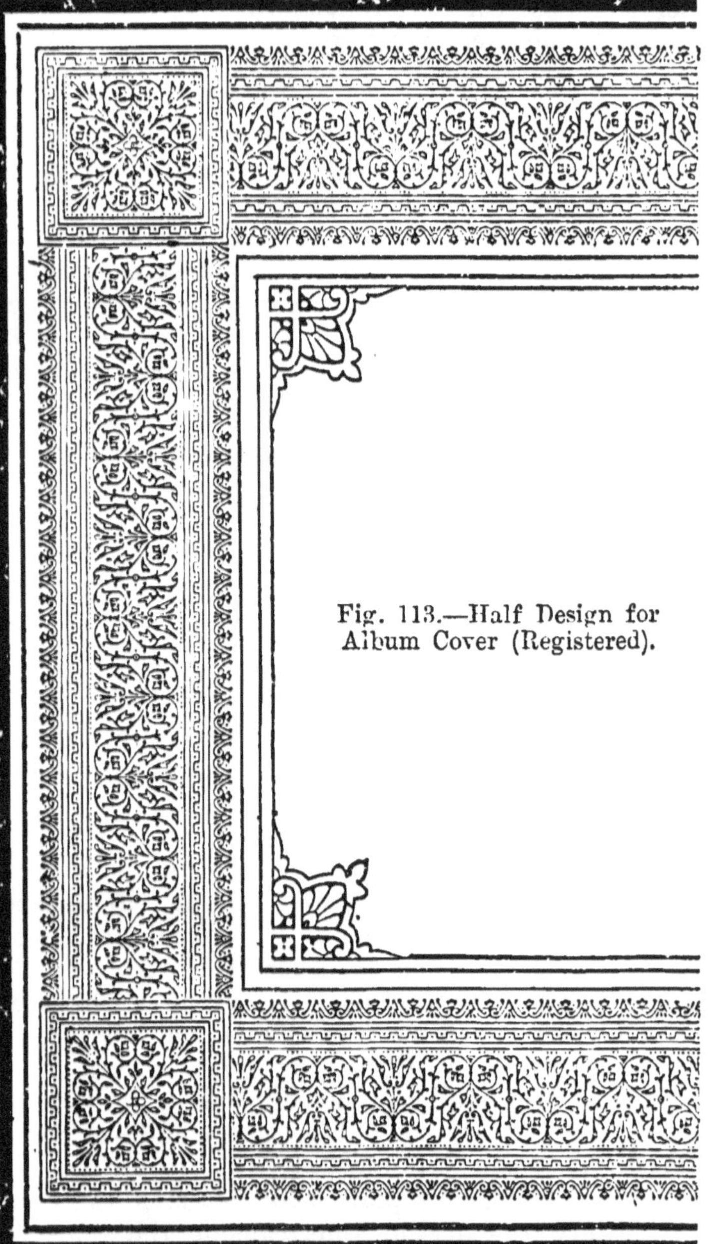

Fig. 113.—Half Design for Album Cover (Registered).

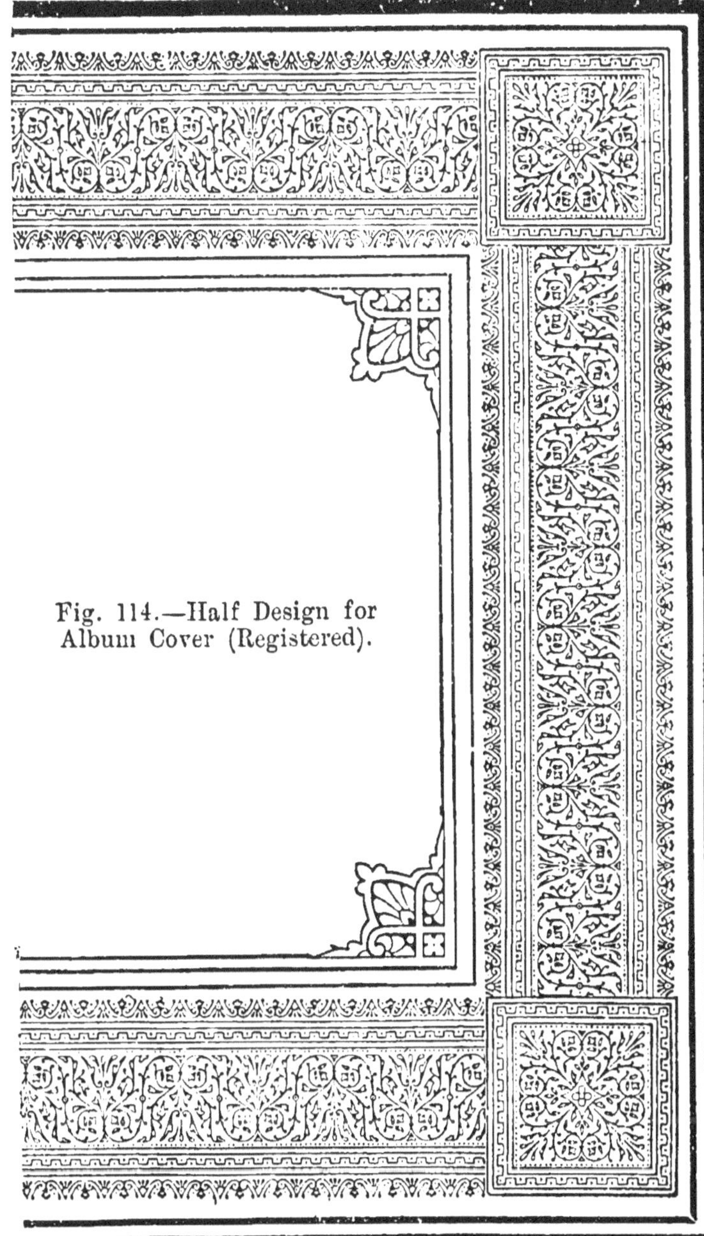

Fig. 114.—Half Design for Album Cover (Registered).

under pressure for a few minutes, take the board out, again turn it over, and place it on the bench. The brown paper may be trimmed off from the outside of the lines with a knife, or it may be left until the whole stamp is set up.

Next place the eight pieces of floral border on

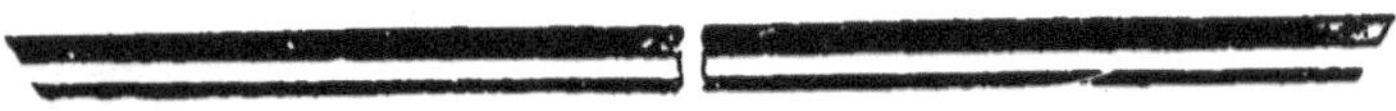

Fig. 115.—Part Border of Cover Design.

the paper inside the lines already adhering thereto ; arrange them carefully, adjusting them with the compasses at equal distances all round. Then take up one piece without moving the other and heat it sufficiently to melt the glue ; pass the glue over it and be sure that it is well glued, place it on the paper in its former position, pressing it down with the fingers, and repeat the operation with the other pieces, again putting the board over it, and turning it over. Then place it in the press as before.

When sufficient time has been allowed, take it out and place it upwards on the bench as before

Fig. 116.—Part Inside Border of Cover Design.

directed. The four corner pieces are then taken, and each piece is glued and placed in position in the manner described for the other pieces. Then if the paper has not already been trimmed from the outside of the lines it must be done now, and if the various pieces have been properly glued and the paper is of the proper quality, there will be no fear of any of the pieces dropping off to give trouble later on.

Cut two pieces of stout strawboard, one exactly the size of one of the boards of the book cover to be blocked, the other somewhat larger each way. With the larger one, set the gauges on the bed of the press, also adjust the bed itself so that the centre of the blocking plate and the centre of the

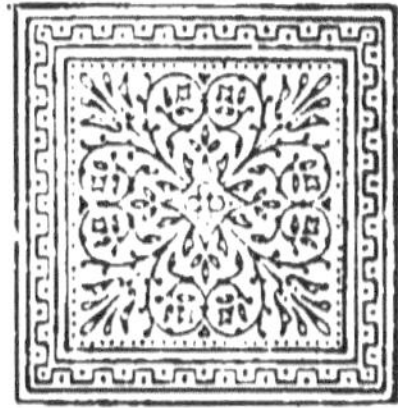

Fig. 117.—Corner of Cover Design.

board will coincide. Now put the smaller board centrally over the larger one and draw two pencil lines at right angles to each other. These lines had better be at the left-hand side and the end farther from the operator. Get four small pieces of board

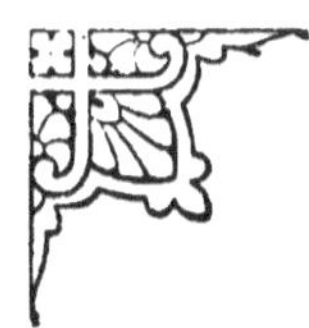

Fig. 118.—Inside Corner of Cover Design.

A (Fig. 119) and attach them as stops to the large board with glue, placing them up to the pencil lines at some distance from each other, two on each line. Press them down and see that they stick well, as the accuracy of the blocking depends upon these little pieces retaining their position. This board and the little pieces glued upon it is called the tray or force.

Put the board that was cut to the size of the

book cover on the tray close to the stops, and on it carefully place the block or stamp, adjusting it to the desired margin. Draw the whole from the bench, taking care that neither the board nor the block shifts, and place it on the bed of the press, adjusting the bottom board or tray to the gauges; then draw or pull the lever so as to make a good impression. Release the lever and withdraw the tray, etc., from the press, place the tray on the bench, remove the block, take up the board, and examine the impression. If this is satisfactory as to position, replace the board upon the tray and the block upon this, and adjust it to the impression already made. If this is done quickly the block should be heated sufficiently to melt the glue. Glue the back of the block well, especially on the heavier parts, insert it in the press as before and pull the lever again, holding it down for a few minutes to allow the glue to become set. On releasing the lever the block will be found adhering to the blocking plate. The tray can then be withdrawn.

An impression from a block of any kind, especially a large one, seldom is equally sharp all over. To make it so, padding, packing, or " making ready " has to be resorted to. First take a good impression on a sheet of white paper, placing it in position on the tray while doing so, and with this as a guide paste pieces of paper on the tray where the impression is light. A number of impressions may have to be taken before a satisfactory result is obtained. The work must, however, be done carefully and completely if good blocking is to result.

The blocking of the cover may be proceeded with now. Assuming this to be of morocco, put the cover on the tray, and make a light impression on it by pulling the lever partly home, at the same time adjusting the pressure so that when the lever may have been pulled to the full extent of the stroke the impression will be as deep as desired and sufficient to make the gold adhere to the leather. The impression is, of course, adjusted by raising or lowering the bed of the press. It is usual to wash morocco leather with paste-water, and this should be done with the cover in hand. The paste-water should be thin and slightly heated; wash over the entire cover with a sponge and afterwards brush lightly with a soft brush, like a cloth brush. This prevents a streakiness appearing while the cover is drying. When dry

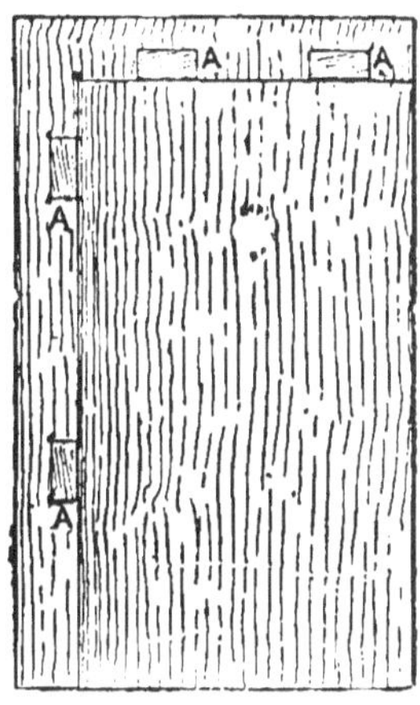

Fig. 119.—Tray or Force.

the entire impression is painted over with glaire, using a small camel-hair brush or pencil.

Glaire (see p. 125) is best prepared by beating up the white of fresh eggs to a thick froth and allowing it to settle, when it will become a clear amber-coloured liquid. At the present time, however, egg glaire is being replaced somewhat by dried albumen dissolved in water; it is unnecessary to give the proportions of each, some operators preferring the glaire thick, others preferring it thin. While the glaire is drying, examine the press and try the blocking plate to see whether it is hot enough. The usual way to test this is to wet the finger upon the tongue and touch the plate with the finger, judging by the amount of hissing which takes place ; experience alone can teach the amount of heat necessary.

The gold leaf may next be put on. Place a few leaves of gold upon the cushion and cut as desired, rub the cover over with a greased rag, that is, a rag with a little olive oil evenly distributed over it and allowed to soak in. Take a piece of gold on the tip or laying-on cotton and press it gently on the cover ; the greasiness from the rag will make it stick. Go on in this manner until the whole design is covered with gold leaf. Then place the cover again on the tray, making sure that it lies well up to the stops, and place the tray well up to the gauges on the bed of the press. Next pull down the lever. It may be necessary to rest a few seconds, or a sharp pull and immediate release may be preferred. When the lever is released, the cover and tray are taken out, the cover is placed on the bench, and the surplus gold is rubbed off with the gold rag, a rag or cloth kept for this purpose only. Any gold still adhering where not desired is cleaned off with rubber. The impression on the book cover should be clear and bright, every part showing the same depth of impression. The other side of the cover is done in like manner, and when that is finished the operator is ready for the next job.

A few remarks may now be given as to the preparation of various other materials for gold blocking. Ordinary bookbinders' cloth requires very little preparation. If the cases are fresh made they will work without addition, but can be washed over with very weak glaire ; use a large sponge and avoid streaks and froth. A spot of olive oil in the glaire will keep down froth. Paste-grain roan can be worked without glaire or other preparation. If the block is a heavy one, blind the impression lightly first and pencil in with glaire. Morocco, grained roan, calf, and russia should be washed with paste-water and glaired as described above. White vellum is difficult to work, but should be washed with size prepared from its own cuttings or vellum scrap; Young's patent size or paste-water may be used. After drying, the impression is glaired as for leather.

Paper and cards, if white and plain, may be washed over with clean glaire. If enamelled, as shop-window tickets or photographic mounts, blocking powder is used. This is generally composed of various proportions of shellac, gum sandarach, and resin very finely ground. It is best bought ready prepared, as home-made powder is not sufficiently fine. The gold can be laid on the cards, if glaired, but if powder is used the gold must be laid on the stamp. Cards may also be pencilled in with glaire like leather. Silk or velvet may be pencilled in with glaire or powdered, and with both the greatest care is necessary. With velvet the impression must be well blinded in first so as to set down all the nap and to get as solid a foundation as possible. Dust in the powder to the impression, or pencil carefully with glaire, avoiding any unnecessary spreading.

For gold blocking cards, proceed in the following manner. Light the gas jets and allow the press to become heated, in the meantime preparing the cards. If they are white, coat or wash them over with glaire, using a soft sponge; spread them out and while they are drying prepare and set up the block. If this is of several pieces it is mounted on brown paper or thin strawboard, and fastened in position on the blocking plate of the press with glue. Then set the gauges on the bed of the press so that the block will come in the desired position on the cards. The gold leaf may next be laid on. Rub the card with an oily rag and lift the gold from the cushion with a piece of carded cotton or a tip and press it gently on the card. Put this on the bed of the press up to the gauges and pull the lever. If the impres-

J

sion on the card is clear and bright, rub off the superfluous gold and clean with rubber. If the cards are coloured, blocking powder must be used instead of glaire. In this case the blocking plate must be taken out of the press and the gold laid thereon, then replaced in the press, and the card, with the powder dusted on, is put in and the lever drawn down as before. The gold will adhere in the same way, but will not be quite so clear as when glaire is used.

Gold blocking on velvet is usually done, as has been mentioned, by first blinding in the impression with a very hot tool or stamp. This must be done thoroughly until the impression shows clear and sharp, and every particle of the pile is well laid down. The impression is carefully painted over with hot isinglass, applied with a small camel-hair pencil. When dry, the impression is painted with glaire, and when this is dry the gold is cut into pieces and taken up on the hot tool and pressed into the impression already made. The gold will adhere and should look clear and bright; any superfluous gold must be carefully brushed away.

For gold blocking the material known as "Kerotol," the varnish sold by the manufacturers of the material should be used unthinned; but there does not seem to be any preparation entirely satisfactory, and Kerotol is a very difficult material to deal with. Perhaps the following mixtures might suit. Take about 1 oz. of Russian glue, break it into small pieces, place it in $\frac{1}{2}$ pint of water, and dissolve slowly. When thoroughly dissolved, carefully drop into it about a tablespoonful of benzine, stirring well. Use this in the ordinary way. The benzine helps to destroy the oil in the material. Or make a saturated solution of sal-ammoniac, and wash up about a dozen articles at a time. Allow them to become surface dry, but no more. Powder may also be used. Be careful with the heat. The sal-ammoniac is worth trying, as it produces good work. It is useless to attempt to work with glaire, as this will chip off when dry.

When book covers are blocked in white metal,

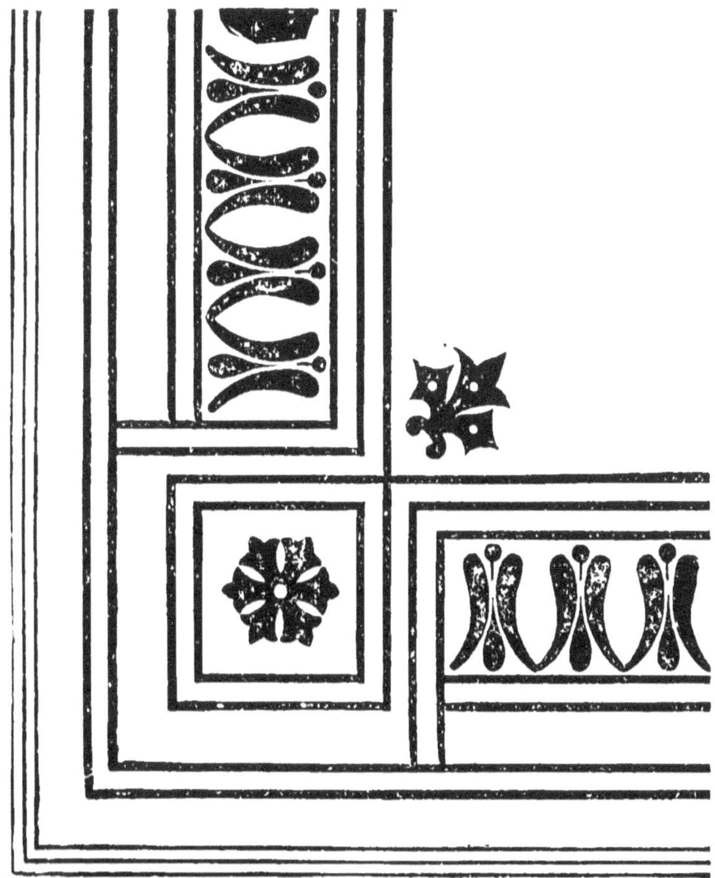

Fig. 120.—Part Design of Hand-tooled Morocco Cover.

aluminium, not silver, is used. It is much thicker than the old-fashioned silver leaf, and consequently is more difficult to work, requiring more heat and a stronger size. A size made from Russian glue, similar to the one recommended in the previous paragraph, has been found to work with cloth of all

grains and with leather of all kinds. As a basis,
break a cake of Russian glue in small pieces, put
them into a jam-pot or other suitable vessel, pour
on about $\frac{1}{2}$ pint of water, and set it on the stove to
melt slowly. In a few minutes, when all the glue
has melted, wash up the cases with this, using a
sponge in the same manner as if glaire were being
used. Try one or two cases, and if the size is too
weak, add more glue.

Owing to its thickness, aluminium must be
treated in a similar manner to Dutch metal, that
is, laid on and worked off immediately. Rubbing
the case with a greasy rag will not cause the metal
to adhere, and the use of more oil or grease simply
results in staining the cloth. Therefore the only
method is to spread it over the space to be blocked
and work off at once. As the metal is very cheap,
it is not worth while cutting it exactly to the size
of the block. After blocking, the superfluous metal
is brushed off, cleaned with a piece of hard india-
rubber, and finally rubbed with a clean duster.

For printing in ink on book covers a blocking
press, an inking roller, a slab (stone or metal), a
pallet knife, and a sheet of rubber about $\frac{1}{4}$ in. thick
called the inking pad will be necessary. After the
block has been set up, the book covers are blocked
blind (a plain impression of a block on a cover is
termed blind), using a warm press. The press is
then allowed to cool, and the preparations for inking are proceeded with. The slab, roller, etc., are
placed conveniently on the bench. Then with the
pallet knife take a small portion of ink from the
tin and daub it on the slab in two or more places.
Take the roller and carefully roll over the ink daubs
so as to spread a perfectly even coating of ink on
the slab and roller. With the roller well ink the
pad, rolling backwards and forwards several times,
and taking up more ink if necessary. Then push
the pad in on the bed of the press and bring the

block down on it gently several times, meanwhile shifting the position of the pad, the object being to ink the block thoroughly. The pad is taken out and a book cover is laid in and impressed by pulling the levers in the usual manner. When the cover

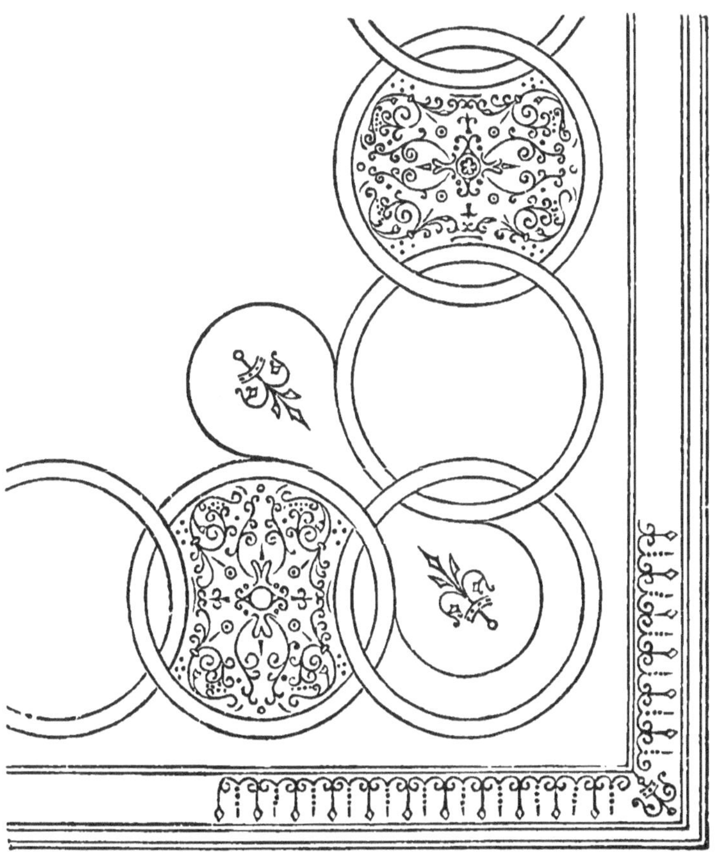

Fig. 121.—Part Design of Hand-tooled Morocco Cover.

is taken out it must be placed on end or hung up on a line to dry. For every impression the pad must be inked before attempting to ink the block, unless this is very small. The pad may be dispensed with if the blocking plate is taken out each time and turned upwards on the bench; the roller can then be used direct. Some presses have an arrangement specially for this purpose called a hinged plate; also there are self-inking presses for dealing with large quantities.

Figs. 120 to 123 show some designs for tooled and blocked book covers. Fig. 120 is a corner and border design to be executed by hand-tooling on morocco; the bands should be made to look heavy. Fig. 121 is a quarter design for the same purpose; in the corner circles there are small ornaments, whilst alternate circles are filled as illustrated; or, instead, all the circles may be filled. Fig. 122 depends for effect entirely on the proper execution of the corners, which are connected by plain lines. Fig. 123 shows a design, dating from 1659, for use on a morocco-bound Bible; perhaps the age of the design is the only feature that recommends it.

The smooth sides of whole-calf volumes are sometimes impressed with a pattern by pressing them between graining plates (Fig. 124, p. 155), this operation being known as graining. One plate is placed against each board of the book, which is then put between pressing boards, screwed down tightly in the standing press, and left for some hours or all night. The most usual pattern is an imitation of the grain of Russia leather. After the book has been pressed with the plates in one position the plates are reversed, and the book again put into the press. The result of the double pressing is shown in Fig. 125. Fish scale, shagreen, and many other patterns may be obtained by the use of engraved graining plates.

It is the custom in some shops, when dealing with half-bound books, for the sides to be put on when the lettering and ornamentation are complete. The inside of the board is lined with the end paper laid aside for that purpose. The other end paper is pasted to the board; care should be taken to make it stick at the joint. The boards are left open to dry, and when sufficiently so the boards are closed, and if the book has marble edges they are burnished with a tooth-shaped burnisher. A sheet of tin or zinc is placed inside and outside each board, and the book placed in the standing press, and the press

Fig. 122.—Part Design of Hand-tooled Morocco Cover.

screwed up more or less tightly, calf allowing of more pressure than morocco. Instead of tins for the outside of morocco books, boards covered with flannel are used to preserve the grain of the leather. When the books are taken out of the press they are polished **up** and looked over for any defects or finger-marks, and when these have been put right the book is completed.

One of the most necessary things in bookbinding is to have clean hands, clean brushes, sponges, paste, water, etc. If this is not attended to strictly, stains and dirty marks are inevitable. Oxalic acid is the only acid used to remove stains. Should a book become stained and dirty, prepare a saturated solution of the acid, pour a few drops into a cupful of water, and wash the entire book cover, using a clean sponge. Do not attempt to rub any spots locally, as rubbing will take the colour out of the leather, and when the leather is of the quality known as fair calf, pink spots will result. In such a case the only remedy is a new cover. The acid solution can be kept in a bottle.

To clean up calf or morocco covers of books, the following method may be employed. Procure a piece of raw rubber, and if this is not soft heat it over the fire or gas flame, for hard, square edges produce scratches on the covers. With this rub over all the gilding on the backs and sides, gently at first and a little harder afterwards ; this should make the gilding clear and bright. Now prepare some paste-water, mixing flour with water till it is as thick as good milk, and apply this with a sponge. Wash over the leather, taking care not to touch the cloth or any of the gilding.

To clean cloth sides, use glaire and a sponge. Have plenty of glaire in the sponge and work quickly in a circular motion, taking care not to go over the same part twice. For some cloths a weaker solution must be used, so add as much water as will make twice the quantity. If this glaire is not properly beaten up, the parts of the book to which it is applied will, when dry, have a nasty glaze, which will turn white and so spoil the appearance.

Oil or grease stains may be removed from cloth book covers as follows. Dip a piece of cotton-wool

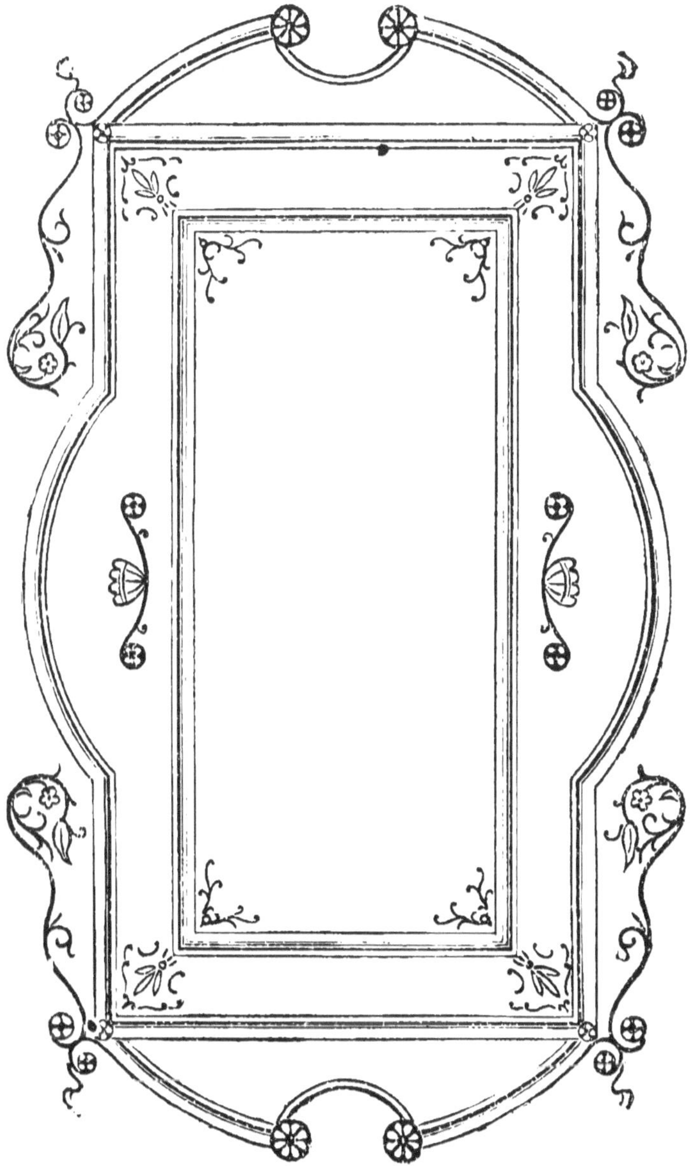

Fig. 123.—Hand-tooled Morocco Cover of Bible.

into benzine and wash over the cover; do not rub
it locally, as this will cause the oil to spread and

leave a ring round the place washed. Move the wool over rapidly; the benzine will sink in the cover and it will appear to have been spoiled, but the benzine will soon evaporate and leave the cover bright and clean. If the stain has been caused by any watery liquid, the colour of the cloth will be destroyed, and there is no effective remedy; but the cover may be improved by washing with glaire—that is, white of egg beaten up. But whichever treatment is adopted, be sure to wash over the whole cover with a quick movement, as much rubbing will only make matters worse.

Egg stains may be removed from leather book covers and similar materials by washing with warm water in which a little flour paste has been mixed. Wash the entire cover, using a clean sponge, but be careful not to rub the gold tooling or lettering. If the cover is of cloth, there will be some difficulty in getting rid of the stains; glaire must be used, and before beginning to wash dilute the glaire with an equal quantity of water. Use a sponge and work in a circular direction; do not rub much or the colour will come out and the surface will have a fluffy, frayed-out appearance. Egg matter that has become hardened will be difficult to remove.

The following method may be tried of removing some oil that has been spilt over a book and causes the letterpress to show through from each side of a leaf. Lay a sheet of blotting paper on each side of a leaf and gently rub a hot iron over it. By this means some of the oil will be removed. Continue this treatment for a considerable time. Another method is to get some benzine and wash the leaves, using cotton-wool. This treatment should not be carried out near a fire or in a very hot room. If the book is badly saturated with oil, the task is hopeless. It may be possible to remove the greasiness, but it will be impossible entirely to remedy the transparency of the leaves.

To remove scratches in morocco, if the skin is not broken, damp the part with hot water, and beat with a clothes-brush, holding it by one end and beating with the point of the other ; this will raise the grain, and if the scratch is slight it will be hidden effectively. If not, while still damp, with the point of a fine needle carefully lift the leather in the scratch, working with the grain, and afterwards damp again and use the brush. If the skin is broken, use the needle and pick up all the edges of the scratch on both sides, rub in a little thin paste,

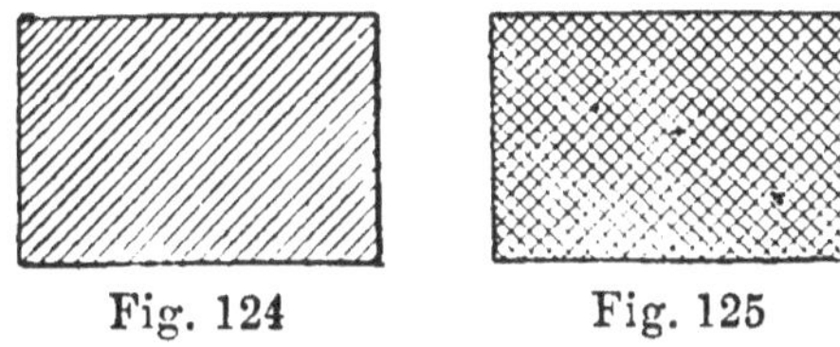

Fig. 124   Fig. 125

Fig. 124.—First Pressing with Graining Plate. Fig 125.—Second Pressing with Graining Plate.

and lay down the edges, using the needle so that each little piece may be carefully replaced in position. Rub off any surplus paste with the sponge. When dry go over it with the needle, stroking where necessary in the direction of the grain of the morocco leather. For calf, instead of the needle and brush, use a bone folder or the handle of a toothbrush. Damp the part first with hot water, rub on a little paste with the finger, and rub well with the folder, taking care to keep it flat or more marks will be made. Wash again and allow to dry. Repeat the operation if necessary. If the skin of calf has been broken, the method of pasting down must be employed, using the folder instead of the brush.

INDEX.